REMEMBERING

# FRANKLIN

COUNTY

# REMEMBERING FRANKLIN COUNTY

## STORIES FROM THE SANDY RIVER VALLEY

LUANN YETTER

Charleston London
THE History PRESS

Published by The History Press
Charleston, SC 29403
www.historypress.net



First published 2009

Manufactured in the United States

ISBN 978.1.59629.610.7

Library of Congress Cataloging-in-Publication Data

Yetter, Luann.
Remembering Franklin County : stories from the Sandy River Valley / Luann Yetter.
p. cm.
Includes bibliographical references.
ISBN 978-1-59629-610-7
1. Franklin County (Me.)--History. I. Title.
F27.F8Y47 2009
974.1'72--dc22
2008045926

# CONTENTS

# ACKNOWLEDGEMENTS

Many thanks to Frank Underkuffler, Richard Mallett, Peter Mills, David Farady, Katie Baum and Dani LeBlanc.

# Chapter One

# PIONEER VIGNETTES

## Queen Elizabeth of Farmington

Elizabeth Henry had an adventurous spirit that matched the times in which she lived. No doubt she was attracted to Stephen Titcomb because she found in him that same sense of adventure and industry that she had herself. Together, their lives would often be hard and perilous but never dull.

When Elizabeth married Stephen she was twenty-seven and he was twenty-four. They both came from comfortable circumstances in Topsham, but they were not content with their easy, predictable lives in coastal Maine. Stephen purchased land on the Sandy River in the forests of western Maine with the intention of making a home for his family in this wilderness. Elizabeth too saw her future to the west and was enthusiastic about the prospect of exploring new territory and making her home where no white woman had settled before. After the wedding, she traded her wedding dress for a flock of sheep, which would serve as the couple's only source of fiber for clothing. While Stephen spent his summers preparing the homestead, clearing land and building shelter, Elizabeth stayed in Topsham in the company of family and friends. In December 1776, the Titcombs' first son, Joseph, was born. Henry followed two years later and then Hannah in November 1780. In December 1780, with two young children and a newborn, Stephen and Elizabeth prepared to set out for the Sandy River Valley to make their new home in the wilderness.

Elizabeth's sisters trembled in fear at the thought of their sister traveling into the dense, forbidding inland forest. Her father thought the plan foolhardy, not only for his daughter's sake, but also the new baby's. "The

The Titcomb family arrives in the Sandy River Valley, 1781. An artist's depiction. *From a mural by Rober Deering, 1939, in the law office of Frank M. Underkuffler, photo by Elizabeth Buckingham.*

child will die before you get there," he warned her. "Carry a spade to dig a grave for the poor thing."

Despite her family's dark predictions, Elizabeth was eager to begin her life in the new world that she and her husband would create for themselves. The pair should have waited for spring to attempt their journey, but they must have thought that their timing was good that December. Perhaps it had been an open winter up to that point and they felt the going would be relatively easy over frozen, snowless ground. However, Maine winters rarely stay open, and this one was no exception. When the group arrived in Readfield, their progress was halted by a violent snowstorm. They took shelter with another family in a log hut while the snow mounted on the path and the wind howled. The snowstorms must have been unrelenting because Elizabeth and her children were forced to stay in Readfield for four months before they could continue their journey west. Meanwhile, Stephen snowshoed on by himself to tend their property and later sap trees. Despite his attempts to oversee the land that winter, bears managed to break into the corncrib and destroy the crop.

Finally, at the end of April, the way was clear for Elizabeth and the children to complete their journey. Elizabeth set out with enthusiasm. Raging streams and a swollen Sandy River were not serious obstacles to her as she eagerly made her way to her new home.

*Above left*: The Titcomb mirror that came with Elizabeth and Stephen when they settled in the Sandy River Valley. *From the collection of the Farmington Historical Society, photo by Elizabeth Buckingham.*
*Above right*: Wooden keg belonging to Elizabeth and Stephen Titcomb. *From the collection of the Farmington Historical Society, photo by Elizabeth Buckingham.*

The arrival of Elizabeth Henry Titcomb and her children heralded the beginnings of the settlement that would soon become Farmington. Of course, Elizabeth's trials did not end with her journey. The family's first year was difficult without the corn that had been taken by the bears. Once when Stephen was clearing land beyond earshot, Elizabeth discovered bears again, this time trying to break into the sheep pen. Determined to guard the wool she had paid so dearly for, she managed by herself to keep them at bay.

Later, after she had given birth to five more healthy children and settled into a spacious and comfortable frame house, her sisters were still shaking their heads. "How did you feel entering the howling wilderness?" they asked her. Elizabeth reflected and smiled serenely. "Oh," she answered, "I felt like a queen."

## The Grinding Trip

In the summer of 1794, the Allen family had a half bushel of corn that needed grinding. The responsibility fell to fourteen-year-old William, who threw the twenty-five-pound bag over his shoulder and trudged five miles on foot to Moses Starling's mill on Temple Stream in West Farmington. But Starling's mill was shut down due to lack of water power. William knew he couldn't go home without the cornmeal that his family depended upon. Samuel Butterfield had water power at the outlet of Wilson's Pond so, in the company of another boy about his age, William threw the twenty-five-pound bag back on his shoulder and headed southwest. The boys walked as far as they could along the river road and then followed a rude path through the woods for several miles until they finally arrived at Butterfield's mill.

By then daylight was almost gone. The boys were tired, hungry and stranded at the mill, fearing they would never find their way back to Farmington in the dark. Samuel and his wife Rachel took pity on them. After grinding their corn, Samuel invited them to stay at his house overnight, and Rachel fed them supper. In the morning, the Butterfields gave their guests breakfast and wished them a safe trip home.

"I always remembered their kindness," William Allen wrote years later, "and afterwards often went out of my way to carry large loads of wheat to his mill."

## A Horse and a Saddle for a Dowry

The Fossett sisters of eighteenth-century Bristol were wealthy and well educated. All of them married sea captains and traveled with their husbands to the ends of the earth, returning to their Maine seaport with treasures from faraway lands. All of them, that is, except Eleanor. Eleanor Fossett was a pretty young woman with bright eyes and a lilting voice. She was every bit as attractive and accomplished as her sisters, yet with her marriage to David Hunter she chose a path far different from theirs. While her sisters traveled the seven seas in search of wealth and adventure, Eleanor's journey was shorter, yet just as adventurous. She traveled west from her seaport home to the settlement of Strong, where she encountered her own challenges and exotic cultures.

At her wedding in 1796, Eleanor's father gave her a horse and saddle. With her wedding gift she eagerly rode west through the forest to the young settlement of Strong. Only a dozen or so families lived in the area when Eleanor and David arrived, and they were joined by David's brothers John and James, while a fourth brother, Thomas, settled in Farmington.

David missed Bristol and his old life in the well-established seaport town of coastal Maine. There, neighbors were close at hand, manufactured goods were available for sale and the whole world was accessible from the nearby harbor. But a subsistence lifestyle was all the settlers of Strong knew. Food came from raising crops, and starvation could be just one bad hailstorm away. Clothes came not from a store but from a long process that began with raising sheep and ended several tedious steps later with a handmade product. The finer things in life, like leather-bound books or sterling silverware, could not be found at all. If the settlers did not bring it with them on their arduous journey through the forest, they did without. Oddly, it was David and not Eleanor who complained about the pioneer lifestyle and entertained thoughts of giving it up and returning to Bristol. Eleanor, however, persuaded him to persevere.

The Hunters' most interesting neighbors were Pealpole (sometimes called Pierpole) and his wife Hannah Susup, full-blooded Indians and the last of their race to live in the area. Hannah did not take kindly to white settlers and usually chose to stick to her own kind. But Eleanor managed to break through Hannah's reserve, and the neighbors became friends. Once some of Pealpole's Indian friends traveled to Strong to visit him and his family and stopped at the Hunters' on their way. The Hunters were happy to invite the Indians into their home and provide them with refreshments before they finished their journey. But after the Indian couple had left, Eleanor discovered that one of her prized possessions was missing. Meanwhile, at Pealpole's house, the visitor was showing off her brightly colored shawl to Hannah. Hannah knew immediately where the shawl had come from and knew her Indian guest had stolen it. The shawl was confiscated and returned to her friend Eleanor.

Through the years in Strong, Eleanor gave birth to eight children and the couple took four more into their home and raised them as their own. Despite tending a farm and raising her children, Eleanor managed to return to her family in Bristol every year. There she would trade stories with her sisters, admiring their grand houses and fine clothing and chatting happily about her own life in a log cabin in the mountains. She would return to Strong with some treasures to adorn her home, some brightly colored silk or rare blue china.

Eleanor liked to use these sea captain treasures to entertain guests, and she was famous for her dinner parties of roast pork and goose. Strong had its own social customs and, as the years went by, more of the hallmarks of civilization appeared. The Hunters were instrumental in establishing the Congregational church in their area and were always active members.

As her many children grew up and had children of their own, and as David's brothers' families did the same, Eleanor became known as Aunt

Birch bark basket belonging to Pealpole and Hannah Sussup, circa 1795. *On loan from Colonial Daughters Chapter of the Daughters of the American Revolution, on display in the Farmington Public Library, photo by Elizabeth Buckingham.*

Top of birch bark basket belonging to Pealpole and Hannah Sussup, circa 1795. *On loan from Colonial Daughters Chapter of the Daughters of the American Revolution, on display in the Farmington Public Library, photo by Elizabeth Buckingham.*

Nellie. No longer the pretty young debutante from Bristol, she became a revered matron of the community, respected for her wisdom and spirit. She remained so until her passing at the age of ninety-eight.

## The Sunday Bear Hunt

On a Sunday in the early 1800s, Wilton settlers were making their way to the meetinghouse when some of them spotted a bear, which aroused much alarm and fear for the local farm animals. Many of the men abandoned their plans to go to church. Instead, they went home to get their hunting dogs and took off for the woods in search of the wild animal.

Nehemiah Hunt, an ordained Methodist minister and Wilton's first preacher, proceeded with his service anyway, preaching mostly to the women and children. Soon he found that everyone was looking out the window instead of listening to him. Their attention was taken by the returning hunters proudly carrying the dead bear. Church services were serious, even sacred, rituals and were rarely interrupted for anything. But the sight of the wild beast was more than anyone could ignore.

"Well," said Elder Hunt. "Let's all go see the bear." Once the poor beast had been inspected and everyone's curiosity satisfied, the people of Wilton entered the meetinghouse and completed their weekly church service.

Chapter Two

# Supply Belcher, The Handel of Maine

Supply Belcher was used to all the amenities that a well-established community in Massachusetts could provide. Yet he abandoned his relatively comfortable existence in Stoughton to carve a life for himself out of the wilderness of western Maine. Rather than relying on the sophisticated network of trade in Massachusetts, which gave him access to all sorts of goods and services, Belcher chose to become a subsistence farmer, living off just what he could make for himself in a land with few settlers, fewer roads and only marginally navigable waters. But Belcher is remembered not just for his ability to survive the rough conditions that challenged all the successful pioneers. He is also remembered as a musician and composer. He was known in his own day, and has been remembered ever since, as "the Handel of Maine."

## Early Musical Influence

Belcher's interest in music began long before he moved to Maine. As a young man in Stoughton, he had studied under William Billings, one of the country's most famous native composers and first professional musicians. Billings was enthusiastic about his music and energetic in spreading the word. He started many singing schools, including one in Belcher's hometown. Belcher was no doubt greatly influenced by Billings. Here was an American with no formal musical training who nevertheless composed music that people loved to sing. Belcher was the son of a doctor, and as a young man he bought a

Portrait of musician Supply Belcher. *From the collection of the Farmington Historical Society, photo by Elizabeth Buckingham.*

tavern that became a gathering place for singers and musicians. While the people of Stoughton had always loved to sing, this was an especially musical period in the town's history, thanks to the arrival of Billings, whose presence helped to kindle a flame. At Billings's singing school, men and women joined together in the evening under Billings's guidance for a group sing. Billings was an enthusiastic teacher and he encouraged others' interest not only in singing, but in composing as well. He was proof that one did not have to be formally trained in Europe to write music. If Billings, a humble tanner, could compose, then so could other ordinary people. Belcher attended Billings's singing school, and it was no doubt here that he got the bug to create his own music. Belcher's own style was influenced by Billings's love of fuguing pieces. Billings described these as compositions "where the parts come in after each other, with the same notes." They were similar to rounds.

## The Belcher Family Moves to Hallowell

In 1785, two years after the end of the Revolutionary War, Belcher and his wife Margaret and six children left Stoughton to move to Hallowell, Maine. The family was part of a wave of newcomers heading into the north woods, lured by inexpensive land and the chance at a new, more independent way of life.

The Belchers settled in Hallowell in the Fort Western area that is now part of Augusta. Hallowell had been incorporated in 1771, and after the Revolutionary War it was a bustling frontier town. Ships routinely left Boston Harbor bound for the young port. They made their way along the Atlantic Coast and up the tidal Kennebec to a bend in the river the Indians called "Bombahook." Wharves lined the shore and the village spread in a ribbon along its banks. Here goods were unloaded and newcomers set foot on Maine soil.

The Belchers spent six years in Hallowell, during which time their youngest child died and Margaret gave birth to two more. Supply quickly established himself as a leader of the community, and when townspeople formed the North Country Militia, he was elected captain. But in moving to Hallowell, Belcher might not have intended to settle there for good. He would have been well aware of the new lands opening up in the inland regions of Maine. Perhaps he made a conscious decision to bide his time at the edge of the frontier, waiting for the best settlement opportunity to arise.

When reports about the Sandy River Valley filtered back to Hallowell, Belcher decided to make his move. The lure of this western region came from its reputation for good, fertile soil. While early settlers would have been well aware of the potential for creating a logging industry and for exploiting water power along fast-running streams and rivers, they knew they must also think about more immediate necessities. No one could venture into the wilderness to create a new home without becoming a subsistence farmer. Consequently, good cropland was essential to the settlers. Early explorers were encouraged by the potential they saw in the river valleys of western Maine and returned to Hallowell with glowing reports.

Belcher's friend John Church, a fellow transplant from Massachusetts, had come to Maine seeking prosperity and had found the Kennebec River Valley to be less than ideal as far as he was concerned. In the fall of 1790, he convinced his friend Supply to investigate the Sandy River Valley area with him. Belcher was thirty-nine and Church was thirty-seven when they made their first journey to the settlement known as Sandy River Township. They were both industrious men, capable and experienced. Belcher had owned a tavern in Massachusetts, Church a blacksmith business. They had much to offer any fledgling settlement in the Maine wilderness, and they determined that this township would have much to offer them.

## INTO THE WILDERNESS

In February 1791, the Belcher and Church families set out on an undeveloped trail that would take them through the wilderness to their new home. They knew that the journey would be difficult in frigid winter conditions, but they must have planned their timing deliberately. Traveling in February would mean beating mud season, a time when the trail no doubt would become impassable. If the families waited until late spring to make their journey when the trail again opened up, they would have been too late to get settled and plant their first crop. And so, with snow swirling around them and drifts rising up in their path, the pioneers headed west out of Hallowell. Along with Supply and Margaret were twins Abigail and Margaret, fifteen; Clifford, thirteen; Samuel, eleven; Benjamin, nine; Mehitable, four; and Hiram, one. Each of the children were to eventually leave their own mark in the town of Farmington, becoming farmers, merchants, teachers, lawyers and doctors' wives. But as they trudged through the snow, bearing their belongings and herding their livestock, they could have little idea of what their futures would be in the community they would help to shape. They must have thought, instead, of keeping warm and keeping on track, bending their heads into the wind. The journey through Readfield, Chesterville and on to Sandy River Township took five days. One of those days, conditions were so bad that the party only made four miles from sunrise to sunset. No doubt they relied on settlements to

Supply Belcher's homestead. *Photos courtesy of the Farmington Historical Society.*

provide shelter. Settlers along the trail from Hallowell to the Sandy River were often visited by pioneers and must have received compensation for providing shelter and meals. Close quarters and meager portions would have met the party, which also included John Church, his wife Susanna (five months pregnant) and his five children. Despite the rugged conditions, the group made it to their destination apparently no worse for wear. Margaret had no chance to investigate her new home before arriving there that February. With all of her worldly possessions piled on a cart and her seven children in tow, she gazed upon it for the first time. What she saw was a settlement far less civilized than the one she had left behind.

## The Belchers as Farmers

When the Belchers moved to Farmington, no town taxes were collected and no town services provided. The five hundred people scattered throughout the settlement belonged to approximately one hundred households, all spread out for about ten miles along the Sandy River from what is now Fairbanks to Farmington Falls, and they had to fend for themselves.

The Belchers had purchased their lot from Seth Greely, who had come to Farmington eight years earlier as one of the first settlers. For seven years Greely lived on his land, probably in a crude log shelter. He had painstakingly cleared trees and begun to farm. Greely most likely realized a nice profit from his labors when he sold his lot to Belcher in 1790 and moved on to Phillips.

The large Belcher family must have moved into the cramped log house on their property, which made up much of what is now the northern part of the village. In the late winter of 1791, they began adjusting to frontier life. At the time the Belchers moved to the area, eight hundred acres were under cultivation. Settlers were growing corn, wheat and beans. Corn was often ground into cornmeal, which housewives such as Margaret would serve as hot cereal or cornbread. Margaret would have had flour ground from wheat and beans to bake with molasses. By this time, gristmills had been established across the river from the Belcher property and also in Farmington Falls. Here farmers could take their corn and wheat to grind it into usable products. Arriving as they did in February, the Belchers probably brought cornmeal and flour with them to last until the following fall. To put meat on the table, settlers depended greatly on wild game. Partridge was a relatively easy bird to shoot and the fowl was a common dish. There were also sawmills along the banks of Temple Stream and the Sandy River. By 1791, many settlers were taking logs to the mill to have them turned into lumber for framed barns. By this time, eight families in the area had the luxury of living in framed houses. The remaining families were living in cruder log structures, concentrating on the basics of survival, clearing land and planting crops before taking time to build more sophisticated homes.

Some of Belcher's neighbors had special skills he could barter for. He could trade corn or wheat for the services of a shoemaker. He could rely upon friend and travel companion John Church for his skills as a blacksmith. The Belchers found no stores in Farmington in 1791. Occasionally, peddlers would journey from Hallowell to sell their wares, and settlers would sometimes make the reverse trip to trade grain for manufactured goods and salt. The trip to Hallowell, the closest center of commerce, took several days.

## The Businessman

Pioneers are often romanticized in history and folklore, and we don't think of them first and foremost as businesspeople. Yet the early settlers were human and their motivations were no nobler than ours. Homesteaders in western Maine hoped to make a profit by their efforts. In many cases, they came from Massachusetts to become land developers, similar in many respects to their modern-day counterparts. When Belcher and Church purchased their new adjoining lots along the Sandy, the location was not considered prime. By 1790, the areas of greatest development had been in what is now Farmington Falls. Also, what we now call West Farmington was seeing the beginnings of commerce. Moses Starling had already erected a mill on the west side of the river and had established himself as a town leader. Starling was the township's first magistrate, given the power to marry people and settle disputes. He was also a carpenter, able to construct buildings as well as sell house lots. Starling had a large and desirable piece of land to develop. He owned frontage not only on the Sandy River but also on Temple Stream, a choice spot for building water-powered mills.

Cathers Drummond (left) with John Church Stewart (right), grandson of John Church. *Photo courtesy of the Farmington Historical Society.*

However, Starling was not the shrewdest of businessmen. When he subdivided his land into house and business lots, he asked exorbitant prices. Perhaps he thought that by sticking to his guns he would eventually get the price he wanted. However, he held out too long. Meanwhile, along came Belcher and Church in 1791, and a year later they were followed by Church's brother-in-law, Hartson Cony. The three bought adjoining lots across the river from Starling and proceeded to subdivide them.

Their prices were lower than Starling's, so the land sold faster. Over the course of the next decade, the tide turned and the center of population and commerce shifted to the east side of the Sandy. John Church sealed the fate of both West Farmington and Farmington village in 1802 when he deeded land to the public for the purpose of building a meetinghouse. Built where the courthouse is today, the meetinghouse established once and for all that the settlement on the east side of the river would serve as the center of commerce and government for the entire town.

## EDUCATION

There was no schoolhouse yet in the young township. Instead, residents made do with private arrangements. During their first year in their new wilderness home, the Belcher children joined others in the area for rather informal schooling. Like most New Englanders of the time, these families put great emphasis on education and did not want to see their children deprived by the lack of an organized school system. Groups of parents most often cooperated in providing space for neighborhood schools and hiring a teacher, often a woman in the summer when farm labor was needed and a man in the winter when they could be spared. Neighborhood children of all ages would gather around a wood stove in someone's kitchen or parlor, making do without desks as they studied their lessons. One of the hallmarks of New England colonial life was the colonists' belief that education was important for all male citizens. By Belcher's time, public education had been mandatory in Massachusetts towns of more than fifty households for over a century. In smaller farming communities where there were no schools, selectmen made sure that all parents were teaching their children to read and write. If parents were not educating their children, sanctions were made and the children could even be taken away from them. Learning was that important.

In an unorganized township such as Sandy River, no such laws applied, but that hardly mattered. All of the area's early inhabitants came from solid

New England backgrounds, and they carried with them a commitment to education. However, this commitment was not made equally to girls and boys. Most New England communities only found room for girls during the summer months, when the older boys were working in the fields.

There were female teachers, but they were not as desirable as men. Much was made of the fact that in 1788 Lemeul Perham Jr. became the township's first male teacher. The fact that the names and circumstances of the earlier female teachers have been lost to history indicates that less was thought of them. It's also obvious how little value was placed on female teachers when we look at the pay scale. In Farmington's early years, women were paid seventy-five cents a week as teachers while men were paid over two dollars a week. Margaret Belcher had received an education in well-respected Boston schools, and it's very likely that she served as a schoolteacher in the Sandy River Township along with her husband, but her contributions were not acknowledged in any of the early histories.

Supply probably taught in his own home. His pupils would have included his five school-age children and probably his neighbor John Church's three children as well. Belcher's other close neighbors, Benjamin and Amy Butler, also had young children who probably joined the group. In the winter, the children might spend their daylight hours, six days a week, with Belcher. Their course of study no doubt followed that of other New England children. They would have read the Bible, the Catechism and the Psalter. From their Catechism they learned prayers such as "Now I Lay Me Down to Sleep," which is still said today. They learned the Lord's Prayer and the Apostle's Creed. *The New England Primer* was a widely circulated textbook in those times, and perhaps a few copies had come with the settlers from Massachusetts. The primer taught youngsters the alphabet with rhymes such as "In Adam's Fall We Sinned All." There was certainly no separation between church and state in these early schools. Christianity and education went hand in hand. However, not all the teachings were religious. *The New England Primer* also contained a picture of George Washington on its front. In the days when Supply Belcher was teaching school, the children learned that Washington was the president of their country. Children also learned the alphabet with the aid of a hornbook. This consisted of a piece of paper pasted to a slab of wood and covered with a transparent sheet of horn. Sitting on straight-backed chairs without benefit even of desks, children in Belcher's house practiced making letters and words on their thick, rough slates. The older children might have had the benefit of a workspace, dipping their goose quill pens into ink made from soot and vinegar and stored in leather bottles, writing on crude pieces of paper. Applied math was taught in early schools along with reading and writing. Belcher would have taught his students facts such as twelve sacks equal a load and ten cowhides equal one dicker.

In the warmer months, Belcher and his older boys could not spare time for school. Beans and corn had to be planted, tended and harvested so that the family would have food to eat the following winter. In the summer months school continued, however. No doubt Margaret Belcher took over the responsibilities in the neighborhood. Her group would have included the girls and the younger boys, and the school days could have lasted longer with the daylight. In this summer school, domestic arts such as sewing were taught to boys as well as girls. Although their children's early education was rather informal, Supply and Margaret Belcher were able to give them a good start. From these humble beginnings, son Samuel went on to become a teacher and Hiram, a lawyer.

Not only did the Belchers find no schools in their new community, but also no churches. One reason for this lack of a space for worship is that the area was settled by members of a variety of different Protestant religions. In the early days, no one sect held sway to organize, build a church and recruit a minister. Margaret, Supply and their children no doubt took to worshipping at home, reading the Bible by firelight in the evening or by daylight on quiet Sunday afternoons. Other reading material would have been scarce. Libraries were a thing of the future and no mail run had yet been established. Newspapers came from Hallowell occasionally and were seized upon eagerly by pioneers hungry for news from the greater world.

## Medicine in the Early Days of Settlement

Between farming, teaching and composing, Belcher's days would have been full. However, he was often called on to do even more; he even practiced medicine. His father, Clifford, had been the first doctor in Stoughton, Massachusetts. This seemed to be all the qualification Belcher needed to fill the role of amateur physician. Perhaps Belcher had accompanied his father on his rounds and picked up a working knowledge of medicine this way. This informal sort of education was in keeping with what many legitimate doctors received at the time.

A man did not have to attend medical school to become a medical doctor in colonial America. After a course of study in college, which included lessons in mathematics, physics and literature, a young man might begin an apprenticeship with a practicing physician. This apprenticeship could last as long as five or six years. In addition to the hands-on experience, the apprentice doctor would be expected to study biology and chemistry on his own. Belcher never pursued such an apprenticeship but, because he was the son of a doctor and a bright man in his own right, the early settlers of the Sandy River Township looked to him when they were sick or injured.

The fact that Belcher was not a real doctor might have made him less zealous in his practice. He might have administered fewer drugs, performed fewer operations and attempted fewer cures than the average colonial doctor. This was probably a good thing. A look at practical medicine of the late 1700s shows that often the "cure" was worse than the disease. For instance, bloodletting, or bleeding, sometimes weakened patients so much they could no longer fight their disease. When Belcher left Stoughton, he might have taken along with him some of the staples he would not find in the remote district of Maine. His baggage might have included a medicine case from his father. In a colonial medicine case were remedies in glass bottles with glass stoppers, mortar and pestle for mixing them and scales for weighing them. Medicines included "glisters" such as jalap, a tuberous root used as a purgative. Purging or otherwise removing bodily waste and fluids was common practice in the eighteenth century. Many doctors held the theory that removing a patient's blood would remove the disease. Belcher's medicine case might have contained some of the metal implements commonly used in those days. For bloodletting, veins were opened with lancets, similar to knives. Eighteenth-century medical practices were often too invasive and medical theory too hypothetical.

Belcher was sometimes called upon to set broken bones. This practice, and any kind of surgery, was a dangerous business in those days. The theory of germs had not been discovered yet and consequently little attention was paid to cleanliness or asepsis. What we would consider a routine operation today could easily have led to infection thanks to unsterilized tools and unwashed hands. Worse yet was the lack of anesthetics. Patients were not put under when bones were set or surgery conducted. Not surprisingly, many died of shock.

In the eighteenth century, people's lack of knowledge about how disease is spread sometimes led to plagues. In large cities such as Boston and Philadelphia, hundreds died from diseases such as yellow fever, which was carried by mosquitoes imported from the Caribbean. For settlers in western Maine, however, plagues were not a cause for worry. While the homesteaders of the Sandy River Township had plenty of challenges to contend with

Fifty-four vials of medicine that belonged to longtime Farmington physician Dr. Albert G. Howard. *From the collection of the Farmington Historical Society, photo by Elizabeth Buckingham.*

in the middle of the wilderness, they were spared the plagues that spread through port cities.

Belcher might have carried an almanac with him to his new frontier home. In it he would have found folk remedies, more useful and gentle than bloodletting or surgery. He probably learned to treat skin infections with a poultice made from fat, honey, mustard, cobwebs and animal dung. Stomach disorders were treated with decoctions of vegetable and berry juices. In a less scientific approach, charms and amulets were also used to ward off disease. And while we may laugh today at the idea, there may have been an important placebo effect to these.

Belcher's efforts to treat the sick and heal the wounded were looked upon with gratitude. He did the best he could with the knowledge and medicines he had to work with. No doubt his duties as an amateur doctor sometimes sent him trudging through the snow in the middle of the night. He was probably called from work in his fields or from his duties as teacher to treat the sick. He was often exposed to infectious diseases himself. For all his trouble he would have been paid with a sack of flour, a bag of apples or a bottle of rum, when he was paid at all.

Belcher never intended to be a doctor and probably would have preferred to spend what little free time he had in musical pursuits, such as playing his violin or composing hymns. In 1794, probably no one in Farmington was happier to see the arrival of Dr. Aaron Stoyell than Supply Belcher. Stoyell not only relieved Belcher of his medical duties but also became his friend and family.

## Farmington Becomes a Town

Belcher and most of his fellow settlers saw the lack of institutions such as schools, churches and newspapers as a temporary condition. Belcher had moved to the Sandy River Township because he hoped the community would grow into a town with all the amenities he was used to in Massachusetts. If it did, his land would become more valuable and his future more secure. By the time the Belchers moved to their new home, there was talk about the township becoming a town. Once incorporated, taxes could be levied and collectively the people could build roads, bridges and schools. Belcher was all for the idea, and by April 1793 he was ready to help make it happen. He got involved in the process of incorporation at its beginning. The first known meeting to discuss the issue of incorporation took place in April 1793 at the home of Belcher's friend and neighbor, Hartson Cony. It was at this meeting that Belcher was chosen to travel to Boston to act as agent for the township. But before he was to take the town's request to the Massachusetts legislature for approval, a controversy arose. A group of settlers in the Farmington Falls area didn't like the way things were going. While the Falls had begun as the center of commerce for the township, focus was now shifting upriver.

Portrait of Elizabeth Titcomb's husband Stephen. *From the collection of the Farmington Historical Society, photo by Elizabeth Buckingham.*

Zacheus Mayhew bringing the weekly mail to Farmington from Hallowell in 1793, with Mount Blue in the background. Artist's depiction. *From a mural by Rober Deering, 1939, in the law office of Frank M. Underkuffler, photo by Elizabeth Buckingham.*

Residents in the Farmington Falls area were not sure they liked these new developments and decided they might be better off breaking away from the northern section and forming their own town along with the area that is now Chesterville. In a separate petition to the Massachusetts legislature, residents including Jonathan Knowlton and Jesse Butterfield made this request. They complained that the long, narrow shape of the present township was "inconvenient." Belcher and his group from the northern half of the township went ahead with their plans for incorporating the whole area. Soon they had swayed property owners who lived between the two centers, such as Robert Gower and Stephen Titcomb, to see things their way. During the summer and fall of 1793, leaders of the incorporation process collected signatures from the majority of settlers. Meanwhile, a separate petition was being circulated in Farmington Falls calling for a separate town, called Parkeford, to be established there.

Both petitions were presented to the legislature in Boston in January 1794. With Belcher as agent for the town, "the North" carried the day and "the South" was not allowed to secede from "the Union." The bill, entitled An Act to Incorporate the Plantation of Sandy River with the Inhabitants Thereof into a Town, passed in both houses of the legislature and was signed into law on February 1. As agent for the township, Belcher had accomplished his mission in Boston. But no doubt he had other business to conduct in Boston that winter as well. As a musician, Belcher was on the brink of becoming a famous composer.

Belcher's motives in volunteering to be the agent for the town were probably twofold. Along with the civic papers he also probably carried with him his musical compositions with the aim of getting them published in Boston. During the years Belcher had lived in Maine, he had somehow managed not only to support his growing family, but also to write music. It was probably during his trip to Boston in 1794 that he found a publisher who was interested in printing his *Harmony of Maine* and distributing it to an audience throughout the new United States.

## *A Harmony of Maine*

In 1794, the same year that he served as agent for his new hometown of Farmington, a collection of Belcher's compositions was published in Boston. He called his book *A Harmony of Maine* and it included psalms, hymns, anthems and fuguing pieces complete with lyrics either taken from the

Book of Psalms or written by Belcher himself. Although his subject matter was most often religious, Belcher's tunes were usually lively. Among music historians they are considered to be a forerunner of the Southern gospel hymn, and Belcher's folksy, vivacious style has since been compared to that of the more recent American composer Stephen Foster. While Belcher never attained the same level of fame as his musical mentor William Billings, he is considered by some to be his equal as a composer. According to University of Maine at Farmington music professor Phil Carlson, who has performed some of Belcher's music, "Belcher's works measure up well with Billings."

Belcher's tunes were composed with the idea in mind that different lyrics might be set to them. Whatever the lyrics, Belcher placed importance on singing them clearly. In the preface to his book he states, "Every word should be pronounced plain and distinct. Singers often fail in this point, by which means half the beauty of the music is lost, the words not being understood."

In the restricted collection at the Farmington Public Library, an original copy of Belcher's *A Harmony of Maine* still exists. The cover is worn and the brown pages are almost too frail to touch, but here we can still see the original compositions that Belcher shared with his fellow townspeople and with music lovers all over the thirteen colonies that had recently become the United States. One of the interesting aspects of Belcher's writing is that the titles to his songs have nothing to do with the lyrics he put with them. Belcher considered the tunes to be separate from the lyrics. Oftentimes a tune was adopted by the listener and different words were exchanged for those in the songbook. This was a common practice, not just with Belcher's music but with much music of the day.

In keeping with the title of his songbook, Belcher liked to use town names for his compositions. This might have been a marketing strategy. Perhaps Belcher figured that music lovers around Maine would be drawn to his songbook if it included a tune named for their hometown. "Readfield," "Turner," "Bath" and "Cumberland" are all songs with a religious theme, but the tunes themselves are surprisingly upbeat. An example of his religious lyrics is in the tune "New Sharon," in which Belcher praises both God and music: "When such as we attempt to sing, The praises of our Heavenly King, His mercies rise to that in view, that still the theme is ever new." Other themes are also represented in Belcher's lyrics. "Unity" is romantic, and the speaker is a woman: "'Twas my beloved spoke, I knew his charming voice. I heard him say rise up my love, my fairest one awake, awake and come away." "Farmington" also is a love song and, here again, the speaker is beseeching a loved one to "come away": "Come my beloved, haste away, Cut short the hours of thy delay; Fly like a youthful hart of roe, Over the hills where spices grow." A hart is a male deer; a doe is a female. It is easy to picture the deer "flying" over the hills of Farmington, but Belcher's reference to spices seems to put the setting somewhere else, perhaps somewhere more tropical and exotic.

One of the few songs in Belcher's songbook that does not take on a place name is "Heroism." In this case, the title does support the lyrics. It is easy to imagine that these lyrics were inspired by the time Belcher spent as a soldier in the Revolutionary War: "Why should vain mortals tremble at the sight of death and destruction, in the field of battle, where blood and carnage clothe the ground in crimson. Sounding, founding, with death groans." Why indeed? It seems to be Belcher's message that "vain mortals" should rise above such scenes and that this is his definition of "heroism."

These are all lyrics Belcher wrote as a fairly young man, when his children were small and his life still unsettled. If he continued to compose music and write lyrics after 1794, they have been lost to time. No further songbooks exist from Belcher. It is easy to imagine that the concerns of his growing family and his growing town began to preoccupy him in the years to come.

## Margaret Marries

In the same year that Farmington became a town, Supply's daughter Margaret married Cornelius Norton Jr. and left the village to make her home in the northernmost section of the New Vineyard Gore, located in what is now the western part of Industry. The area was then untouched wilderness, and Cornelius's lot was in the most isolated section of this territory.

Cornelius had first seen this mountainous area when he came with his father from Martha's Vineyard at the age of eighteen. While surveying their new property, he and his father stayed in Farmington, possibly with John Church, who took in boarders. There is no doubt it was then that he met Margaret. Cornelius purchased a section of land from his father and set about clearing it in the spring of 1791. His home of Martha's Vineyard was an island that had become overpopulated. The prospect of unsettled land excited Cornelius and, perhaps because he had lost two brothers at sea, he had no qualms about leaving behind the life of a fisherman. Perhaps he and Margaret already had an agreement about their future. This might have been his motivation for all the hard work it took to make his section of the

Gore livable. Before he married Margaret, Cornelius cleared some of his land in order to plant crops and build a house. This task required amazing strength and endurance. The old growth trees, tall and wide, did not yield easily to an axe. Once he had made a clearing wide enough to allow for a breeze, he burned off more of his land and, like others in the area, probably planted corn, wheat and rye. Cornelius then set to building a house, probably with the help of his father, who settled on adjoining property to the south. The house was built from unmilled logs, probably with a roof of hemlock or spruce bark. To keep the cold winter air out and the warmth from the fire in, cracks between the logs were caulked with moss on the inside and clay on the outside. The chimney was made with stone and a clay mortar.

Margaret was the first of Supply's ten children to marry. She had been born in 1776, the year the United States declared independence from England, and married in 1794, the year Farmington became a town. Margaret did not stay in Center Village Farmington to enjoy the civilized aspects that came with incorporation. Her life had already consisted of a series of moves during her eighteen years, each one to an area more remote than the last. She had been born in Stoughton, a well-settled community near enough to Boston and Cambridge to seem cosmopolitan by colonial standards. She had left there with her family to live in Hallowell, which was then a bustling port, growing rapidly but marked by the rough edges that characterize a frontier town. Then at fifteen, an age when girls appreciate social activities, her father moved the family to the Sandy River Township, a new settlement that did not yet have any of the refinements of society such as clubs, schools or even churches. Now her union with Cornelius would take her even farther into the wilderness.

With the log cabin built and a crop ready to harvest, twenty-two-year-old Cornelius Norton married Margaret Belcher, eighteen, in August 1794. Although their life in the wilderness was difficult, the couple persevered. A year after their marriage, Margaret gave birth to a son they named Cornelius. Harriet and Supply soon followed. When Cornelius's father was no longer able to farm his land, the family moved onto his property and built a large two-story home. No longer in a log cabin and no longer quite so isolated, Margaret's life became easier and here she gave birth to Sophronia, Clifford, Margaret, Abigail and Lydia. All eight of Margaret and Cornelius's children lived to adulthood, and the farm they had carved out of the wilderness flourished.

The Nortons were leaders in the growing community of Industry. They were active in the Congregational church and Cornelius served several years as chairman of the board of selectmen. Before her death at the age of sixty-three, Margaret must have been able to look back with satisfaction on the life she had made for herself.

## Farmington's First Town Meeting

In 1794, Supply Belcher carried the petition for incorporation of the town of Farmington to the state capital in Boston. In January of that year, the legislature passed the bill that officially made Farmington a town. It was then possible for citizens to levy taxes and make improvements in their community. Farmington's first town meeting was held in April 1794 at the home of Dr. Thomas Flint, a doctor who eventually set up practice in New Vineyard. At the time of incorporation, he was living in Farmington near what is now the fairgrounds. In those days it seems that doctors sometimes needed to supplement their income with other labors. In Flint's case, he operated a general store and sold potash for fertilizer.

Women did not vote and probably were not even welcome at early town meetings. The first order of the day for the men of the community was to cast their votes for governor and lieutenant governor of Massachusetts and for treasurer of Lincoln County. These votes did not raise any controversy and the men were unanimous in their choices. The next act of business hit closer to home. Townspeople came up with seventeen different offices needing representatives in an official capacity. Some of these, such as fence viewer and hog reever, perhaps did not demand a lot of time.

Belcher, however, was elected to the position of clerk, a job that demanded knowledge of forms and procedures and a skill for organization. Along with Belcher, Solomon Adams took on responsibilities for the town, becoming the first moderator. Adams was probably granted this position in part because he had been one of the earliest explorers to the region. Also in positions of power that first year were the three men elected as selectmen and assessors. One of these was Peter Corbett, who, along with Adams, had explored and then settled in the Sandy River Valley in the early 1780s. Corbett had the distinction of building the first framed house in the township and was already enjoying this luxury while most of his fellow townspeople still lived in log cabins. Corbett was to hold his post as chairman of the board for seven years. Also on the board was Ezekial Porter, who, like Belcher, had come from Hallowell. He had settled on the west side of the river in 1790 on what has ever since been known as Porter

Hill. Not only did he name the hill, but he also gets credit for coming up with the name of the town. The third member of the board was Enoch Craig, whose ties to the Sandy River Valley went back to its earliest days of settlement. Craig did not have a framed house, but he was known for having the best log house in the township. These men, with the help of many others in lesser positions, were charged with operation of the new town of Farmington. Their first act was to call a second town meeting for May, and at this time the citizens got down to business.

Money was still measured in British pounds rather than in American dollars, and the men of Farmington voted to raise £300 for improvement of roads; £600 were voted to establish schools. With these decisions made, Belcher and his fellow townspeople went on with their daily tasks of maintaining food, shelter and clothing, satisfied in the knowledge that civilization, in the form of laws, had come to their community.

## DR. STOYELL ARRIVES

Twenty-six-year-old Aaron Stoyell came to the Sandy River Valley from Connecticut and had no family ties to Massachusetts, so he was an outsider to the community by any standards. But because he was well educated, no doubt he was made to feel welcome. During his first winter in his new home in West Farmington, Stoyell, who was unmarried, made his living by teaching school. Because they lived on opposite banks of the Sandy River, Belcher and Stoyell probably did not become well acquainted right away. Eventually they discovered they had much in common. Both of them taught school, but more important was their shared interest in medicine. In fact, it turned out the young man from Connecticut was a medical doctor who had studied and apprenticed in the town of Northbridge before moving into the wilderness. Nothing could have made Belcher happier than to discover a professional medical man in the Sandy River Township. Belcher had been called upon all hours of the day or night to care for the sick and injured. These duties, as well as his responsibilities as farmer, schoolteacher, politician and composer, were taking their toll. His wife Margaret, for one, must have felt that Belcher did not have enough time to call his own. It might have been those nighttime emergency calls that accounted for the fact that no children were born to Supply and Margaret during these years. Margaret had given birth to a baby every couple of years during her marriage, until the couple's early years in

Farmington. Then there was a five-year span in which no new babies were born in the Belcher household. When a qualified young man came along who could relieve him of some of his more demanding duties, Belcher was eager to accommodate him. Stoyell might have intended to start his medical practice in West Farmington, since the west bank of the river rivaled the east in growth and commerce at the time. It was Belcher, no doubt, who convinced Stoyell to move to the other side and arranged for his friend and neighbor John Church to sell him a parcel of land in this fledgling settlement.

Dr. Stoyell opened his office near Church's log house, part of which served as a store. Church was located in the area where the courthouse stands today. Stoyell's new property was near the corner of Broadway and Main. His move to the east side of the river was one of the events that marked the beginning of what was to become downtown Farmington. Dr. Aaron Stoyell's move from West Farmington to Center Village in 1794 put him squarely in the neighborhood and under the influence of John Church, Hartson Cony and Supply Belcher. These enterprising pioneers had invested in the east side of the Sandy River with hopes of developing the property into a thriving town. Stoyell's move to this particular spot in the new town of Farmington helped to cement their plans. Stoyell and Belcher became great friends, and when Belcher's wife, Margaret, gave birth to her ninth child in 1795, the couple gave her the middle name of Stoyell in honor of their new neighbor. Supply and Margaret weren't the only ones taken with Stoyell. Their nineteen-year-old daughter, Abigail, liked him too, and within a year after Stoyell moved to the village, he and Abigail were married. Stoyell became not only a friend to Belcher, but a son-in-law as well. Stoyell was a popular doctor and Abigail enjoyed some of the luxuries that came with marriage to a professional man. No one in the fledgling settlement of Farmington lived a particularly easy life. Shelter was still primitive, winters were harsh and communication with centers of commerce and government such as Boston, or even Hallowell, were difficult. Yet by Farmington standards, Abigail and Aaron led an enviable existence. He was a well-respected physician and never lacked patients. Consequently, the family didn't lack food. In the early days, it was more likely that Stoyell was paid in wheat or corn than in cash. After Abigail married Aaron, she was still within easy walking distance of her parents and younger siblings, so she had the opportunity to see them frequently. She remained in the same neighborhood with family friends John and Susanna Church. The population of Center Village was growing rapidly and Abigail found herself in the middle of an active community. While twin sister Margaret had left the growing town of Farmington behind, Abigail's adulthood was spent in the relative refinement of town life.

## The Federalists and the Republicans

There are times in Farmington's history when the town seems far removed from the world of national politics. At other times, issues come to a head and the political climate here seems a microcosm of national affairs. One of these times occurred in 1798, when Supply Belcher ran against Ezekiel Porter to represent Farmington in the Massachusetts legislature. As party politics emerged as a force in the nation's capital, they also served as a rallying point in the fledgling town of Farmington.

At the national level, John Adams became president of the United States in 1798. During George Washington's presidency, Adams had been vice president. While Washington himself opposed the formation of two political parties, factions developed during his presidency. Adams became a leader of the Federalist Party. Members favored a strong central government, the development of manufacturing and leadership from the upper class. Federalists had opposition from the Anti-Federalists, soon to be known as the Democratic Republicans, or Republicans for short. Thomas Jefferson led the Republicans. He and his party believed that the Constitution should be strictly interpreted and the powers of the federal government severely limited. He had a much more populist view and felt that people from all classes should take part in the government. Jefferson defended the interests of the farmer against those of the merchant.

By 1798, Belcher probably felt that his homestead was well enough established that he could afford the time to travel by horse to Hallowell and then by ship to Boston for legislative sessions. By then his oldest son, Clifford, was twenty, and along with eighteen-year-old Samuel and sixteen-year-old Benjamin, could take care of the farm in his absence.

Belcher ran for the office of representative as a Federalist. This means he aligned himself with John Adams and Alexander Hamilton, taking both a pro-business and pro–federal government stand. Probably because party sentiment was running high, Belcher encountered opposition. Ezekiel Porter ran for representative on the Republican ticket, which probably means he sought to champion the farmer, prevent special consideration for manufacturing interests and reduce federal government control and taxes.

Two years previously, Adams had carried the day on the national level under the banner of the Federalists. In Farmington in 1798, townspeople were poised, wondering if the Federalist or Republican candidate would triumph in their community. Belcher defeated Ezekiel Porter to become Farmington's first representative to the Massachusetts legislature. The election had been a hard-fought one and Republican supporters gave Porter forty-five votes to the Federalists' fifty-seven for Belcher. He might have been pleased with the victory when he headed to Boston in May for his first session, but he was to find that opposition to him and his party would not stop at the election. The federal government, led at the time by Federalist President John Adams, soon imposed a tax on each of the states. Because Adams and his party pushed for a strong federal government, they sought to control the states by controlling the purse strings. Massachusetts was socked with a tax bill of $260,000, which had to be collected from landowners not only in the lower counties, but in the District of Maine as well. Probably because of his new status as state representative, Belcher was appointed by the legislature to serve in the unpopular job of district assessor. It was up to him to see that this new tax was collected from the townspeople of Farmington, New Sharon, Anson, Wilton and Chesterville. Not surprisingly, there was opposition to Belcher's assessment from members of the Democratic Republican Party, who believed in states' rights and favored a weak federal government. In December 1778, a warrant was issued for a special town meeting to discuss these issues.

Meanwhile, Belcher and twenty other townsmen signed a petition of protest. Since Belcher's is the first signature and since most of the controversy revolved around him, it is reasonable to assume that he was the author of the protest. He complained that assessors had been prevented from doing their job. He charged the Republicans with deliberately encouraging dissension and warned that their protest could lead to dangerous anti-government sentiment. These local Federalists protested the special town meeting by staying away, which ultimately enabled the Republicans to carry the day.

The Republicans' overall objection to this assessment might have been on principle. They no doubt opposed the entire idea of a federal tax. However, at the meeting they took issue with more local concerns, implying that Belcher had not been fair in his assessments and complaining that the assessor should have been picked by local selectmen rather than the legislators. At this special town meeting, a committee of three was chosen to discuss these grievances with Belcher, who quite diplomatically told the committee that he had the best interests of his constituents at heart. If townspeople wanted

Center Meetinghouse, erected in 1803. *Photo courtesy of the Farmington Historical Society.*

him to resign, he would go quietly. A vote was taken among the Republicans in attendance, and all forty there voted for Belcher not to attend the spring session of the legislature, in effect calling for his resignation. The following spring, Republican candidate Ezekiel Porter was elected representative, but in the following year, townspeople returned Supply Belcher to the post.

## CLIFFORD BELCHER AND JOSEPH TITCOMB GO INTO BUSINESS

As the eighteenth century gave way to the nineteenth, Supply Belcher began to slow his pace of activities while his children began to take an active role in local affairs. By 1800, Supply was fifty years old, still healthy and energetic but ready to take a back seat to the ambitious exploits of his children and other second-generation settlers. Supply owned a large acreage just to the north of what is now the downtown district. Around 1800, he sold a portion of this to his future son-in-law, Joseph Titcomb. This marked the beginning of the transformation of his property from frontier farm to village neighborhood. Joseph Titcomb was the oldest son of early Farmington settler Stephen Titcomb. He had come to the Sandy River Township as a boy and then left to attend boarding school at Hallowell Academy as a teenager. In 1803, at the age of twenty-seven, he opened a store on his upper Main Street property. The following year, he had company when Supply's son Clifford opened a store just to the south of him. At the beginning of the 1800s, there was other activity in the area as well. Farmington's first meetinghouse was erected on the site where the courthouse stands today. Brothers Timothy and Thomas Johnson, sons of settler Thomas Johnson from Martha's Vineyard, opened a store where the District Court Building is now. That made three stores in the neighborhood to serve the growing Center Village population. Five years after purchasing his store, Joseph Titcomb married Supply Belcher's daughter Mehitable. He was thirty-two and already well established in business. His bride was twenty-one. Joseph built a large, gracious house on Main Street the same year he married Mehitable. Within the next thirteen years, the couple had six sons.

Meanwhile, up the street, Clifford continued to run his store and also made money buying and selling real estate. It wasn't long before he was one of Farmington's most prosperous businessmen. Clifford waited until he was well established in business before he took a bride. When he finally decided to marry at the age of thirty-three, he found a refined woman of twenty-nine named Deborah Allen. We don't know when or where Clifford met Deborah, but she was not from the Farmington area. She was the daughter of a minister and a descendant of a prominent Cambridge family named Fuller. Like his brother-in-law, Clifford built a house for his new bride next to his store on Main Street. In the years that followed, Clifford and Deborah had six children, and no doubt they played with, and were close to, their Titcomb cousins.

Clifford had good business instincts and became one of the wealthiest men in Farmington. Despite his success, he remained down to earth. Growing up with the hardships of life on a frontier farm seemed to leave a lasting impression on him. He was not the intellectual or the artist that his father had been, but he did inherit Supply's common sense and capacity for hard work. These traits served him well as he made the transition from farmer to merchant. Clifford and his wife Deborah were happy and prosperous until tragedy struck in 1832. It was then, at the age of fifty-four, that Clifford took ill and died. He left Deborah with six children to care for, the youngest only nine years old. His oldest daughter, Caroline, was probably at boarding

Nathan Backus's stage line to Hallowell, 1808. Artist's depiction. *From a mural by Rober Deering, 1939, in the law office of Frank M. Underkuffler, photo by Elizabeth Buckingham.*

school when her father died. Caroline was a bright young woman who benefited from her father's wealth and her mother's Boston connections. One of Caroline's second cousins, Margaret Fuller, was also her classmate and close friend and became a famous author, critic and social reformer. Caroline herself married well and was able to provide some stability for her mother after her father's death. Two years after Clifford died, Caroline married Nehemiah Abbott. He was older than Caroline and already had a successful law practice in Belfast. Four years after Clifford's death, Deborah sold their home and store on Main Street and eventually moved to Belfast to be with her oldest daughter.

Supply and his wife Margaret were still alive and still living on the homestead when Clifford died. They lived to see Clifford's sons Clifford and Samuel become lawyers and daughter Caroline marry an attorney. They probably took an active role in caring for and comforting their younger grandchildren after Clifford's death. Supply and Margaret also lived to see Clifford's house and store lots sold to a stranger. Within their lifetime, other subdivisions of their original settler's lot fell out of the hands of family members as well. In 1820, Mehitable Belcher's husband Joseph Titcomb decided he'd had enough of town life. Joseph was a farmer at heart, a devout member of the Congregational church and a no-nonsense kind of man who felt that village life provided too many temptations for his children. When he moved his family to a farm outside the village, he sold his store on Upper Main Street to his brother John.

## Paul Revere's Bell

On a warm July day in 1809, Belcher received a letter from a Boston silversmith named Paul Revere. The name probably sounded familiar to him. Supply might have heard of Revere as a Patriot who drew political cartoons and designed the first Continental currency and the state seal of Massachusetts. He might have known that Revere had been a major in the state militia and commander of Castle William in Boston Harbor. Belcher didn't think of Revere as a messenger and the phrase "midnight ride" probably didn't pop into his mind. Revere did not become a mythical figure until Henry Wadsworth Longfellow immortalized him in poem several decades later. At this point, Revere was a businessman and silversmith with a problem and he hoped Belcher could help because, as a representative to the Massachusetts legislature, it was part of Belcher's job to listen to complaints and intervene when he could. Revere had made and delivered a bell for the new Farmington Academy, but he hadn't been paid for it. He wrote:

> *The 24 of November last we delivered a bell to a young gentleman who said he was implaced to purchase a bell for the said Academy (by the Trustees of Farmington Academy) of about 500 lbs. The one we delivered weighed 495 lbs. at 42 cents came to $207.90. He said the Trustees would send the pay early in the spring. As we have not seen him since nor heard from the Trustees we will thank you to require them to write us whether, they, received the bell or that they gave any person order to purchase the bell.*

Belcher didn't have to investigate much to determine that the academy had indeed received the bell. Most of the trustees were local men and he was well acquainted with them. Belcher knew they had the bell. He also knew they didn't have the funds to pay for it, or to build a building to put it in. We don't know what reply Belcher made to Revere's complaint, but it was a period of tough times all over, and the academy was no exception. From a business standpoint, the Farmington Academy—precursor to the Normal School, Farmington State Teachers College and the University of Maine at Farmington—got off to a rocky start. Farmington Academy was the twelfth to be granted in the state. Like townspeople in many Maine communities, residents of Farmington in the early 1800s felt a need for an institution of higher education in their town. The academies functioned both as training schools for teachers and preparatory schools for students wishing to go to college. They accepted women as well as men and offered a course of study in language, arts and sciences. Men of Farmington such as attorney Nathan Cutler and farmer Church Brainerd showed foresight in wishing to build such an academy in their town. By doing so, they established Farmington as a seat of higher learning, and it has remained so ever since.

However, in the year 1807, when trustees first made plans to build such a school, they were immediately the victims of hard times. This was due to a national recession that followed swiftly on the heels of Thomas Jefferson's Embargo Act. At the time, England and France were at war and both countries were harassing the United States over issues of trade. In response to this harassment, Jefferson banned American merchants from any kind of foreign trade. By doing so, he hoped that France and England would suffer from the loss of raw goods from the United States and become more amenable to allowing free trade. The results were disastrous for the entire Northeast economy. Merchants, shippers and shipbuilders suffered, as did farmers who lost foreign markets for their crops. It was on the eve of this economic turmoil that the trustees of Farmington Academy set out to build a school and purchase a bell, based on the promise of a land grant from the Massachusetts legislature and generous pledges from area residents. These plans quickly ran into problems. Doctor and merchant Thomas Flint donated $100; Ezekiel Porter, $91.21; Eliphalet Bailey, $78.59. This list goes on, amounting in total to fifty-five contributors and more than $3,000. Some of this money was deposited in a bank account where trustees let it sit, earning interest for several years. Other contributors had offered "notes of hand," which probably amounted to IOUs. But when the embargo put an end to U.S. trade, it also hurt the struggling farmers and merchants of the Sandy River Valley. Consequently, not as much money was collected for the construction of the school as organizers had hoped.

Nevertheless, work began on the structure in 1808, and it was in that same year that Paul Revere delivered a bell for the school. When Revere wrote to Supply Belcher a year later to complain about nonpayment, there wasn't much Belcher could do to help. The trustees were stubbornly hanging on to what money they had collected. A year later, Revere wrote to the academy directly, admonishing it for its long-delinquent bill. "You know you have a bell, you know who it was purchased of, who purchased it and the terms it was purchased upon…and you all know it is not paid for. What are we to think of the Gentlemen who composed the Trustees of Farmington Academy?" he chided them.

Revere wasn't the only person to suffer financially at the hands of the academy. The school's first preceptor also complained of nonpayment. James Hall taught at the academy in 1812 and 1813. The following year he wrote to an acquaintance, "Your humble servant was once unfortunately preceptor of Farmington Academy and what I am about to say is not hearsay. They owe me a considerable sum of money but they have used every means in their power to swindle me out of it, and by the want of which I have been greatly distressed. Neither am I the only person whom they have cruelly abused." We don't know if poor James Hall was ever compensated for his cruel abuse, but we do know that eventually the trustees got around to paying Paul Revere for his bell. To his contemporaries, Revere was just another Boston war veteran and craftsman. In this case, he was a craftsman trying to collect on a bad debt.

## The Legal Tradition Begins

Supply and Margaret's youngest son, Hiram, became the most successful of all his children. He had the benefit of an education at Hallowell Academy and then apprenticed with a Maine attorney before becoming a lawyer himself in 1812. He set up practice on family land along Main Street and, when he was twenty-seven, married his late brother Samuel's widow Evelina and became guardian of his late brother's four daughters. A year after the marriage, Hiram and Evelina's son Hannibal was born. In 1820, the couple settled their growing family in a large, comfortable house across the street from Hiram's law office. Hiram's brother-in-law, Joseph Titcomb, had built the house a few years before and when Joseph decided to move to a farm on a hill above the village, Hiram eagerly jumped at the chance to buy the property.

Together Hiram and Evelina had six children. Four of them—Hannibal, Abigail, Susan and Margaret—lived to adulthood. Hiram's political career began to take off when he served as a state legislator. After Hiram established himself in law and politics, he jointed the Congregational church. When the church was first organized in 1814, his sister Mehitable Belcher Titcomb had been one of the founding members. In 1826, Isaac Rogers came to town to serve as pastor to the fledgling congregation. Under his leadership, which lasted for nearly fifty years, the church grew and prospered. Membership steadily increased though the 1800s. In 1828, the year Hiram Belcher joined the church, he was one of thirty-seven new members.

Hiram served as mentor for several family members who decided to follow his footsteps and become lawyers. In the 1830s, his nephews Samuel Belcher and Stephen Titcomb served as apprentices in his law office. Samuel eventually opened his own law office in Farmington (and was later joined by his son), while Titcomb went on to practice law in East Wilton. In 1839, Hiram's son Hannibal joined his father's law practice.

The mark that Supply's descendants left on the legal community in Farmington is noteworthy. Hiram was the only one of Supply's children to become a lawyer or even to study at an academy. He set a precedent for succeeding generations to enter the legal profession. In 1885, for instance, a couple of generations removed from founding fathers like Supply, there were nine lawyers practicing in Farmington. Four of them were Belchers.

Supply didn't live to see Hiram reach the peak of his political career. In 1846, when Hiram was elected to serve in Congress, it was the crowning achievement of his public life. When Hiram went to Washington, D.C., to represent Maine, he became one of the most famous politicians in the history of Farmington.

## The Pioneer Musician Dies

The year was 1836. It was the year that Betsy Ross died and Winslow Homer was born. Texas became a republic; Charles Dickens wrote *The Pickwick Papers* and Ralph Waldo Emerson penned his essay on "Nature."

In Farmington, parishioners were busy erecting both a Free Baptist and a Congregational church. There was talk in the air about the western part of Kennebec County breaking away to become a county of its own, with Farmington as the shiretown.

It was in 1836, on a warm day in June, that Supply Belcher quietly passed away at the age of eighty-five. As one of the last of the early settlers, his death marked the end of an era. By that time, there were few people left who had taken an active role, as Supply had, in the formation of the town. At the time of his death, Supply was still living on what was left of the settler's lot he had purchased in 1791. He had already passed on most of his property to his children, who had built houses of their own along Main Street. Because Supply had already sold or given his offspring most of his land, which was his most valuable possession, he had little else to leave anybody.

Consequently, the only real benefactor of the Supply Belcher estate was his grandson Enoch, who had been born on the Belcher homestead in 1811. His father was Benjamin, the Belcher sibling who had stayed at home to tend the farm while all the others went off to build new homes of their own. Enoch had grown up in the same house as his grandfather and the two became close. When Enoch was thirteen, his father died, and grandfather and grandson became even closer. At the time of Supply's death, Enoch was a grown man of twenty-five. He had proven himself capable enough to run the farm and sensitive enough to care for his elderly grandmother. Supply left his property to Enoch under the condition that Enoch care for Margaret for the remainder of her life.

Enoch's younger brothers, Hiram and Benjamin, each received $150 from Supply's estate. To the rest of Supply's numerous descendants he left token amounts. One dollar each went to his four living children. One cent each went to the heirs of his deceased children. On the surface, these small sums seem to be worse than nothing at all, as if Supply were taunting his descendants with such small change. This was not the case, however.

Supply's son Hiram was an attorney and had no doubt advised Supply on the proper way to make a will. Leaving each of his descendants a small sum showed that he acknowledged them and didn't forget to put them in the will. This habit of leaving token amounts to any descendant who might have a claim on the estate was a customary legal procedure. Both Supply's son Hiram and his son-in-law Thomas Hunter served as executors of his will, which indicates that there were no hard feelings among family members about Supply's decisions.

No doubt all of his children, grandchildren and great-grandchildren mourned the death of their patriarch, as did the rest of the Farmington community. With the death of Supply Belcher, Farmington lost one its last founding fathers. And yet two hundred years after he penned the music for *A Harmony of Maine*, his work lives on. Musicologists study his tunes, choral groups sing them and orchestras perform them. The exuberant hymns of Belcher and other early American composers left a lasting impression on American music, and their style can be traced though the frontier singing schools of the nineteenth century to the minstrel shows of the early twentieth century. Even today's genre of Americana music owes a debt of lineage to homegrown music that began with Belcher and his American contemporaries.

## Chapter Three

# THE OLDEST COUNTRY STORE

Mary Gower was a farmer's daughter and a farmer's granddaughter. She was born on the family homestead that her grandfather Robert had claimed when he became one of the Sandy River Valley's first residents in the late 1700s. When Mary was twenty, her life on the farm ended. It was then, in 1821, that she left home to marry thirty-year-old storekeeper Thomas Croswell.

By the time of his marriage to Mary, Thomas had been in business in Farmington Falls for five years. Being a merchant in the early 1800s was far different from being in business today. Thomas and Mary dealt not so much in currency as in produce. In catering primarily to subsistence farmers, Croswell's offered only the products that were impossible, or at least difficult, for its customers to make themselves. Among the goods in Croswell's store were indulgences such as rum, brandy and snuff; fabrics such as cambric; and dies such as indigo. In order to obtain these goods, farmers offered whatever they had in surplus, such as homemade butter, homegrown and dried beans and apples, sheep pelts or shaved shingles. The Croswells ended up with many more of these goods than they could use themselves, so they in turn traded with wholesale suppliers located on the Kennebec River in Hallowell, an important port for boats full of goods traveling to and from Boston. A trip from the Falls to Hallowell was no easy journey and took days by ox cart. When Thomas's sons were old enough, they made the trip to Hallowell for supplies. Sometimes, the stock in the store would be depleted before they returned. When they got back to Farmington Falls, they would often find customers eager for the latest shipments of rum and molasses.

Before even unloading the giant hogsheads from the cart, the boys would begin filling jugs for townspeople thirsty for rum or hungry for molasses to go with their baked beans.

For fifty years Thomas Croswell ran his store in Farmington Falls and for forty-five of those years Mary was by his side. Mary's grandparents had been a founding family, yet she had watched all ten of her brothers and sisters leave the area, most of them heading west. Some of her own children followed suit. Eldest daughter Mary moved to California, James to Minnesota and Micah to Illinois. At the age of twenty-two, Andrew joined the gold rush.

Lured by stories of riches, twenty-two-year-old Andrew set out from Farmington Falls in the summer of 1849. Six months later, after a trip around Cape Horn, he landed in the boomtown of San Francisco, where he quickly found work as a carpenter. "Wages were high at the time," recalled Croswell, "and we got all the way from $10 to $15 per day."

But there was a catch. While Croswell was making good money by nineteenth-century standards, he was paying twenty-first-century prices. "Commodity prices were high so that savings were not great," he continued. "A hard-boiled egg in a restaurant brought $1 and a pair of coarse boots cost $40."

Restless after a winter of carpentering, Andrew made up his mind in April to head into "the gold diggings." He took passage on a sloop going up the San Joaquin River to Stockton. From there he loaded his tools and clothes on an ox cart and walked sixty miles to the Sonora area, where he and his partners set up camp and proceeded prospecting. Success did not follow immediately. Several weeks' work resulted in only twenty-five cents' worth of gold.

But suddenly Andrew and his partners cut a new trail and struck it rich. In four days they mined $500 worth of gold. Even split four ways, the find yielded a huge reward for a few days' work. But the vein ran out and Andrew spent two more weeks prospecting with no luck. All in all, Andrew spent his summer mining for gold and made only about $125—deducting the cost of his tools and travel, even less. Like many miners before him, he decided he could capitalize on the gold rush in better ways than by prospecting. He returned to Stockton, where he once again took up carpentry. Within a couple of weeks, he made more than he had mining for gold.

Few miners made a fortune in the gold rush, but Andrew knew one who did. He had met D.G. Greaton, his wife and daughter in the mining camps around Sonora when they were poor and hopeful just like everyone else. Years later, Andrew ran into Greaton in Stockton. He was then independently wealthy, spending his time breeding horses on his palatial ranch. Greaton claimed to have made over $100,000 mining for gold, and he credited his deceased wife for his good fortune. She had been clairvoyant, he said. "He could put her in a trance by the waving of his hand," Andrew related. "In this condition he took her from claim to claim which she declared 'No good,' until finally they struck one that she insisted was the best ever seen. So he went to work there and struck it rich."

No doubt a sixth sense would have been a good thing to have during the California gold rush. Without one, most prospectors, like Croswell, worked hard, made a living and eventually returned home without a fortune, but with tales of adventure.

After several years in California, Andrew moved to Minnesota. At the age of thirty-five, he married Lizzie Rich in Monticello, Minnesota. Coincidentally, Lizzie's father was from Dixmont, Maine, and the couple eventually returned to Maine. Meanwhile, Andrew's older brother Thomas had stayed behind to help his father with the store. His sister Susan had also entered into trade. Needless to say, it was not common for a woman to go into business for herself in the mid-1800s. A directory from 1885 lists forty-four businesses in the Farmington area, and only three (all of them millineries) were run by women. It seems shopkeeping was in Susan's blood, having grown up with it. Susan remained single and ran her shop for nearly fifty years. Hats were considered essential apparel in those days, and women were constantly redecorating them. A simple hat could serve for many years but would go through several overhauls along the way. Consequently, Susan's millinery shop kept many accessories in stock. Ribbons, laces, buckles, plumes, flowers and birds filled her shelves and were used by women to create unique effects. Susan did her best to keep up with current styles and trends. She traveled to Boston and New York frequently on buying trips, and she would have been pleased to know that her savvy as a buyer was recognized years later in a historical exhibit. In 1934, the Chicago department store Carson, Pirie Scott and Co. featured some hats from Susan's shop in a historical fashion display.

Susan once threw a birthday party for a young girl in Farmington Falls. The details of who that girl was, and just exactly when that party took place, have been lost. However, the party itself became a part of Farmington Falls legend because, as party favors, each of the young guests was allowed to choose and decorate her own hat.

Susan had a head start in running her own business, but when brothers Tom and Andrew inherited the general store, they were quick to catch

Susan Croswell in California at one hundred. *Photo courtesy of the Farmington Historical Society.*

up. The Croswell brothers took over the ownership from their father, Thomas Sr., in 1866. By the time their father retired, Andrew was thirty-nine and Thomas forty-one. The retail trade system had become much more sophisticated than the barter system Thomas Sr. had started with in 1816. By the mid-1800s, Farmington and neighboring Chesterville had developed quite a reputation for building carriages. Enterprising local carriage makers in the area had begun to supply not only their neighbors but also customers in all corners of the state. Charles Watson was one of many successful carriage and sleigh makers in the area. He took over the Franklin Pulp Mill in Farmington Falls in the 1880s and used the water power to propel his planing equipment. In 1890, he built fifty-two sleighs and made the woodwork for about forty-eight more. By 1890, Watson had competition in the trade from Benjamin Watson, who built a shop across the road. A.P. Carville and Lemuel Hodgkins were also successful carriage makers in the Falls. This thriving local industry proved to be a boon to the Croswell Store. Local manufacturers made the bare-bones chassis but needed to purchase many of the accessories for their vehicles. The Croswell Store provided these, and this sideline proved to be a very lucrative one. While Thomas Sr. had gotten by trading products such as molasses and rum for produce such as beans and eggs, his sons now grossed over $100,000 a year in the carriage accessory trade.

In addition to thriving in business, Tom also took an active role in politics, becoming a state representative in 1872. He and his wife Harriet had no children. Andrew and his wife Lizzie had five children, including twins named for the partners, Thomas and Andrew. It might have been fitting in a literary sort of way if these namesake twins had taken over the store from their father and uncle, but that was not to be. They headed to California, while their sister Mary became a doctor. It was Andrew's first-born son Clyde and his second son Ernest who carried on the Croswell tradition.

Around the turn of the century, Tom and Andrew both retired, as did their sister Susan. After retirement, Susan cared for her brother Tom, then a widower with no children. While Clyde and Ernest took over the family store, Ernest's wife took over the hat shop. They marked the third generation of Croswells in trade in Farmington Falls, and they inherited a thriving business still bolstered by the busy carriage makers in town. Carriage makers could not keep up, however, with the advent of the "horseless carriage." The introduction of the automobile and mass production put an end to Farmington's thriving carriage business; consequently, Ernest and Clyde watched the decline of their accessory business.

Years later, the attic above Croswell's Store could tell the story of their glory years. In an article in 1945, local historian Blanche Applebee described the treasures still stored there: "Here are sleigh yokes, sleigh hangers, iron steps, cabinet woods, prefabricated panels and insets, whiffletrees, upholstery buttons, fender boots, whip sockets and dozens of other deluxe items, many of them in unbroken dozen lots, and a few in the original gross containers." The unused items spoke of a booming trade suddenly gone bust.

In the face of a changing economic climate, Clyde and Andrew managed to diversify. As the demand for locally made carriages lessened, the partners turned their sights to locally grown produce. They established an apple distribution business and found markets nationally and internationally. They also branched out into the farm machinery business. In the 1920s, area farmers began to realize the benefits of the Fordson tractor. Along with tractors came other innovations in farming and farm machinery. Clyde served the agricultural community as distributor of these new inventions.

Farmington resident Ina Porter Turner worked at the store when Clyde and Ernest were in charge and the place was in its prime. "I can see now, so nice and shiny," she recalled in 1995. "It was the cleanest, most beautiful

Apple label, circa 1920. *Photo courtesy of the Maine State Museum.*

store." Turner remembered details that probably had remained the same for a hundred years, like the hitching posts for horses and the dried beans sold in bags and tied with twine. Ernest Croswell was "very fussy and dapper," said Turner. He would go next door to his well-kept federal-style home for his midday meal, and when he would return to the store he would reach inside his suit coat for a quill with which to clean his teeth.

In 1930, as the Great Depression was beginning, Ernest died following an operation. He was sixty-three. His brother Clyde continued operating the store alone for three years. He then asked Ernest's son Robert to join him in the business. Robert did not seem to be on a path toward taking up the family tradition. He had always had an active interest in electronics and had been an early ham radio operator. After attending high school in Farmington, he had gone on to get a degree from the Massachusetts Institute of Technology and then pursued a career in radio in Connecticut.

But as a Croswell from Farmington Falls, he must have been very familiar with the retail trade, and he must have known that he would be expected someday to take over the reins of Croswell's Store, just as his father, grandfather and great-grandfather had before him. Robert married, raised a daughter, a son and stepson and became a Boy Scout leader. He also served on the school board. He was a well-respected member of the community and, in the summer of 1948, he even became a hero. It was then that two thieves attempted to break into Croswell's Store, and one in particular was later sorry he ever tried. Using his expertise in electronics, Croswell had rigged up an alarm system between his store and home. Around 2:00 a.m., he heard the alarm go off. He hurriedly got dressed and grabbed a gun while his wife phoned the sheriff. Armed with a twelve-gauge shotgun, Croswell staked out the side door of the store, counting on

Robert Croswell as a baby. *Photo courtesy of the Farmington Historical Society.*

the arrival of the police to flush out the intruders. When officer Kenneth French showed up, two men bolted from the side door. From eighty-five feet away Croswell shot one of them in the back with a spray of birdshot. The burglar evidently had a pistol in his hand that fell to the ground as he was shot. As he crawled on hands and knees to retrieve the pistol, French tackled and subdued him. Croswell and French quickly realized that the man had been badly wounded by the birdshot and called an ambulance. Croswell was standing outside the store, shotgun still in hand, when the ambulance arrived. "Dim those lights. This is still a battleground!" he told the driver. Croswell was excited, not only because he had caught his thief in the act but also because he knew a second burglar was still on the loose; however, they never caught him. At the hospital, the thief, Brewer resident Andrew Gallagher, required a blood transfusion, and officials observed that his shirt looked "like a sieve" from the birdshot. It was soon discovered that he and his accomplice had broken into the store by forcing open and crawling through a window. They had gone for the safe, where they tried to break into an inner compartment and were evidently in the process of removing bolts when they realized they had been discovered and attempted to flee. No one ever questioned Croswell's right to shoot the intruder in the back. The fact that Gallagher was carrying a loaded .38-caliber revolver was probably indication enough that Croswell was defending himself as well as his property.

For ten more years Robert Croswell served as storekeeper to the village of Farmington Falls. But in 1958, he made the momentous decision to close the doors on Croswell's Store. It couldn't have been an easy decision for him to make, knowing that his ancestors had always run the store in town. For 142 years the Croswells had furnished the townspeople of Farmington Falls with the provisions of everyday life and been involved in the area's most prosperous businesses. By 1958, it was the oldest family-operated store in New England. But Robert was not cut out for only storekeeping. He had a talent for engineering and a degree from MIT. After twenty-four years as a storekeeper, he decided it was time to get back to his chosen field of engineering. In 1958, the Croswell family closed the door to its store for the final time, and another tangible link to Franklin County's pioneer history began to fade.

Chapter Four

# THE STEVENS FAMILY SETTLES UPCOUNTRY

Caleb Stevens and his family knew hunger and isolation in their home on Stratton Brook, far from the nearest settlement of Kingfield. For years the family struggled to establish a foothold in the mountainous border region of Maine, and ultimately they survived and succeeded.

Early lumbermen and developers Gillman and Redington induced Stevens and his family to leave the relatively civilized settlement of Kingfield for the untouched wilderness of the Dead River area in 1818. Gillman and Redington felt their investment would be more secure if they had year-round settlers on their property. Caleb was forty-three years old at the time and a veteran of the War of 1812. His wife Sally was thirty-six. They were strong and healthy and felt up to the challenge of life in the wilderness beyond the outpost of Kingfield. The family was given one year's provisions and a choice 160 acres of Dead River land in exchange for permanent settlement. Stevens arrived a couple of months after Gillman and Redington to choose his site and prepare for his family's arrival. He made his first trip into the wilderness on foot, carrying all the gear and tools he needed in a pack. Alone, he cleared land, cut hay and built a house twenty by thirty feet, then returned to Kingfield for his wife and children. Caleb and Sally set out for their new home with nine children: sons Paul, Henry, William, Prince and Jeremiah and daughters Mary, Azubah, Sarah and Acbsah. Paul was the oldest at eighteen. On the first day of their journey, they traveled to the Carrabassett Valley and camped for the night near what is now the access road to Sugarloaf USA. The next day, they arrived at their new home.

The Stevens family had some company in the Dead River Valley during their first few months. Redington and Gillman's crew logged the area through the early part of the winter and, after a successful operation, they returned to Waterville in January. Caleb and Sally must have been sorry to see them leave, for it meant that they were now truly left alone in this vast mountain wilderness, with the harshest part of the winter yet to come. The family survived those cold months alone, but their toughest challenges followed in the spring. The family had been counting on an early crop of wheat, but that first crop was a failure and the family was forced to watch their provisions disappear as they waited out the second crop. All alone in the wilderness, with their food stores gone, Caleb and his wife faced the prospect of watching their family starve to death. Desperate to find food, Caleb remembered that the logging crew had told him of provisions they had stored before they left. They said they had stashed two bags of flour, some pork and molasses under a boat hung up in the trees at Grand Falls. The spot was thirty miles downriver from the homestead and Caleb hesitated to check it out. Could he leave his family in their already weakened state? Could he be sure he would find the provisions? The trip was a treacherous one, and even if he made it wild animals might have gotten to the food already. After consideration, Caleb decided he had no choice. He and his son Paul made the journey in their log canoe. At the end of the day, they arrived at Grand Falls, and there in the tree was a boat. In the boat Caleb found the food, untouched and edible. The pair had to spend the night on the river and then return upstream the next day with the provisions that would save their family from starvation.

With a second crop in the ground and food in the cupboard, Caleb left his family for Kingfield, where he hired a horse and took the trail that followed the Carrabassett River and the Kennebec to Skowhegan. There he worked in a sawmill, earning more provisions to take back to his family. Loaded with bushels of wheat and other necessities, the horse's load was too heavy to take a rider on the return trip, so Caleb had to lead the horse as well as carry part of the provisions himself. After he returned the horse to Kingfield, he had to continue to his homestead on foot, carrying what he could and leaving a couple of bushels of flour behind for a second trip. Weather was on their side, and the second crop proved abundant for the Stevens family. With this harvest, the worst of their suffering was over and their future in the wilderness appeared much brighter. As time progressed, their situation became more comfortable and secure. Sally gave birth to Caleb, the first white baby to be born in the area.

In December 1819, the Stevens family had a visitor to their remote outpost. Benjamin Allen had intended to settle near the Stevens family, but after a treacherous journey from Kingfield he changed his mind. Allen traveled on foot as far as Stratton Brook without incident but, as night fell, he decided to rest there until daybreak. He tried to light a fire with the flint and steel he had with him, but he was unable to create a flame; this is when his troubles began. Without the warmth of a fire, Allen took refuge in a haystack for the night and tried to fight off the cold, but his wet feet froze stiff. The Stevens house was a mile away, and somehow, the next day he made his way there. The Stevens family gave him food and shelter, but Allen's toes could not be saved. They had to be amputated, and quickly. Caleb had no choice but to do the job himself using a paring chisel.

Allen survived his ordeal, but he abandoned his efforts to settle in the Dead River area and returned to Kingfield, and so the Stevens family was left alone again. Sally did not see another woman for two years after moving into the wilderness. She had the company of her husband and nine children, but no neighbor to visit or see at church services or rely on when her next baby was due. Sometimes even her husband was not around. As the family farm was getting established, he often had to provide food for his family by returning to work at the sawmill in Skowhegan. The isolation must also have been hard on the older children as they became young adults and began to think of courting and marriage.

But after three years alone on Stratton Brook, the Stevens family was joined by other homesteaders, including the Reed, Proctor, Keen, Allen, Bartlett and Staples families. Although the Stevens family must have been an independent bunch, no doubt they were relieved to have neighbors after so many years. By the time Sally had her final three sons—Caleb, Consider and Seriah—she had the company of other mothers to share in the trials and blessings.

In 1823, Caleb built a sawmill on Stratton Brook to accommodate the "building boom" taking place along the Dead River. By 1824, enough families had settled in the area to begin a school. Sessions first took place in the Stevenses' barn and later the settlers built a log schoolhouse. A gristmill followed so that settlers could grind their crops to make meal. By 1826, a handful of families had formed a community where residents could reduce their burdens by depending upon one another and even find time for an occasional celebration. The first Independence Celebration took place that year and included a liberty pole and an abundance of new rum and molasses. In 1830, Charles Eustis began to develop a large tract of land north of the

The Stevens family in 1901. *Left to right*: Kate Smith Stevens, Caleb Dalton Stevens, Mark Stevens, Roxie Stevens, Caleb Dalton Stevens (age eighty). *Photo courtesy of the Dead River Historical Society.*

Stevenses and their neighbors, and after that Stratton Brook was no longer the northernmost settlement in the area.

In 1857, Eustis became a township and the first real commerce began to take place. Stores slowly began to appear in the community. Around this time, Charles Bemis started a store in Eustis Mills, and the location remained a general store for several years under a variety of owners. In 1862, Daniel Paine built a shingle machine at Eustis Mills. Blacksmith shops, repair shops and hotels followed, serving the transient population of loggers.

Caleb and Sally survived and prospered as the first settlers of Eustis. Every one of their twelve children lived to adulthood. The pioneers watched their children grow up and leave the homestead. Their oldest son, Paul, settled in Sidney. Henry moved to Illinois and eventually his family lost contact with him. William lived his whole life in Eustis. Mary married a man from Starks and moved there. Prince married Assenath Staples, the daughter of another early settler, and eventually they moved to Iowa. Azubah married and moved to Waterville. Jeremiah settled in New Portland and fought in the Civil War at the age of fifty. After Sarah lost her husband and son in the Civil War, she lived as a widow on a farm in Hebron. Acbsah married

Daniel Randall and settled in Kingfield. Caleb married a local girl and lived in Eustis his entire life. Consider moved to Iowa. Seriah died while still in his twenties. All of the Stevens siblings made their living as farmers. The trials of life in the wilderness did not diminish the health of Caleb or his wife. He lived out his years in Eustis and died at the age of eighty; Sally lived to be eighty-five. They were buried in the town they helped to establish.

Chapter Five

# ODDITIES

## Wilton's Giantess

Sylvia Hardy was always a bit unusual, but growing up on a Wilton farm in the 1820s, family and friends could never have predicted her future. She was a twin, which probably accounts for her low birth weight of five pounds. Unfortunately, her brother died when the pair was only four months old. Sylvia was not only the healthier of the two, but she was also physically advanced by any standards and already walking by the surprisingly young age of eight months. She was advanced for her age mentally as well. Legend has it that she started attending school before she had even turned three.

When Sylvia was seven, tragedy struck her family when her father died. Her mother, unable to support Sylvia on her own, sent her to the Eatons, a wealthier Wilton family. As a child, Sylvia remained small for her age and very slim. In fact, her classmates teased her about her little hands; they called them "bird claws." But when Sylvia was twelve she started to grow. Many adolescents shoot up at this age, but Sylvia was different. She didn't stop. Soon she was taller than all her sisters, then taller than her mother and even taller than her father had been. When she was fifteen, she left the Eaton house and boarded with a succession of other local families.

She kept growing.

Eventually, her mother remarried and Sylvia moved in with her and her new stepfather.

She kept growing.

Sylvia Hardy photographed in Wilton by D.K. Jewell. *Photo courtesy of the Wilton Farm and Home Museum.*

After she finished school, she kept growing. By the age of twenty-one she had reached her full height. Reports vary about just how tall she was. Some say she was more than seven feet tall. Some describe her as "near eight feet high." Local writer John Willard, who knew Sylvia personally, scoffed at those figures. "I believe the public would like to see a reliable account, after seeing so many exaggerated accounts of her," he wrote in the *Maine Farmer* in 1867. Sylvia's full height was six feet, eight inches, he asserted. "The truth in this case is large enough," he said. "It needs no stretching."

Sylvia became known as "the Maine Giantess." And while Willard reports that she was "of modest and retiring habits," she was eventually persuaded to join P.T. Barnum's American Museum in New York City. Here she was put on display along with the Albino, the Bearded Lady and the Fat Girl. With this entourage she traveled across the country and to Cuba. Sylvia may not have like appearing in public as an oddity. A *New York Times* review of one of her appearances describes her expression as "perplexed." Simply walking down a street was probably difficult for her. Willard notes that anyone seeing her for the first time reacted with open "astonishment." And it's easy to

Sylvia Hardy, from an etching probably used in newspapers when she was with the P.T. Barnum Museum. *Photo courtesy of the Wilton Farm and Home Museum.*

believe that, like most of us, she would have felt self-conscious about being so tall. Yet her height enabled her to make a good living. In later years she bought a house in Wilton village for her mother, who once again was a widow. After losing her father and bouncing between a variety of families to earn her keep, Sylvia was probably happy to have some financial stability in her adult years. Life as a giantess couldn't have been easy. Yet it was her height that gave her a living and the opportunity to see the world beyond her hometown.

## POLLY DERBY FULFILLS A PROPHECY

A friend from New Hampshire once predicted that someone in the Derby family would become a centenarian, and Polly Derby was sure the prophecy would apply to her. Along with the prophecy, Polly had other reasons to believe she would live a long life. Her father had lived to be ninety-two, her mother ninety-five and her grandmother ninety-seven.

Polly was born in 1791 in Lancaster, New Hampshire, when the country was new and the Bill of Rights had just been ratified. When she was ten, the year Thomas Jefferson became president, she moved to Westminster, Massachusetts. She never married, but at the age of thirty she moved to Maine, living first in Gray, then in Temple and finally Wilton. She saw Maine separate from the Commonwealth of Massachusetts and the Confederacy separate from the Union. She lived to see the invention of the typewriter and telephone, baseball and basketball. Through her lifetime, the population of her country grew from three million to fifty million people.

When she reached her eighty-eighth birthday, friends and neighbors who had adopted her as their own gathered at her home in Wilton to help Aunty Polly celebrate. Falling the day after Christmas, Polly's birthday was easy to remember. The next year, the group assembled again for her birthday. The party became an annual Wilton event, with more friends and neighbors joining each time. Everyone wished her well and marveled at her longevity. And with each passing year, they wondered, at least to themselves, if that birthday party would be her last.

Polly rose at four o'clock every morning, even in darkest winter. She was cheerful and outgoing; she loved company. In 1885, Grover Cleveland became president. In 1889, North and South Dakota became states. In 1890, the Women's Suffrage Association was established. Aunt Polly lived on. She became the oldest person in Wilton. After the Christmas of 1891, Wilton celebrated Aunt Polly's 100th birthday. At the time only five other people in the state had reached the century mark. The prophecy fulfilled, Aunt Polly passed away the next November.

## THE ENCHANTED DEER

In the late 1800s, one particular deer kept hunters in Franklin County so baffled that they claimed it was enchanted. The doe caught the attention of half a dozen hunters in Madrid, including the mayor of Lewiston, during the fall of 1895. Mayor Noble had an excellent opportunity to shoot the

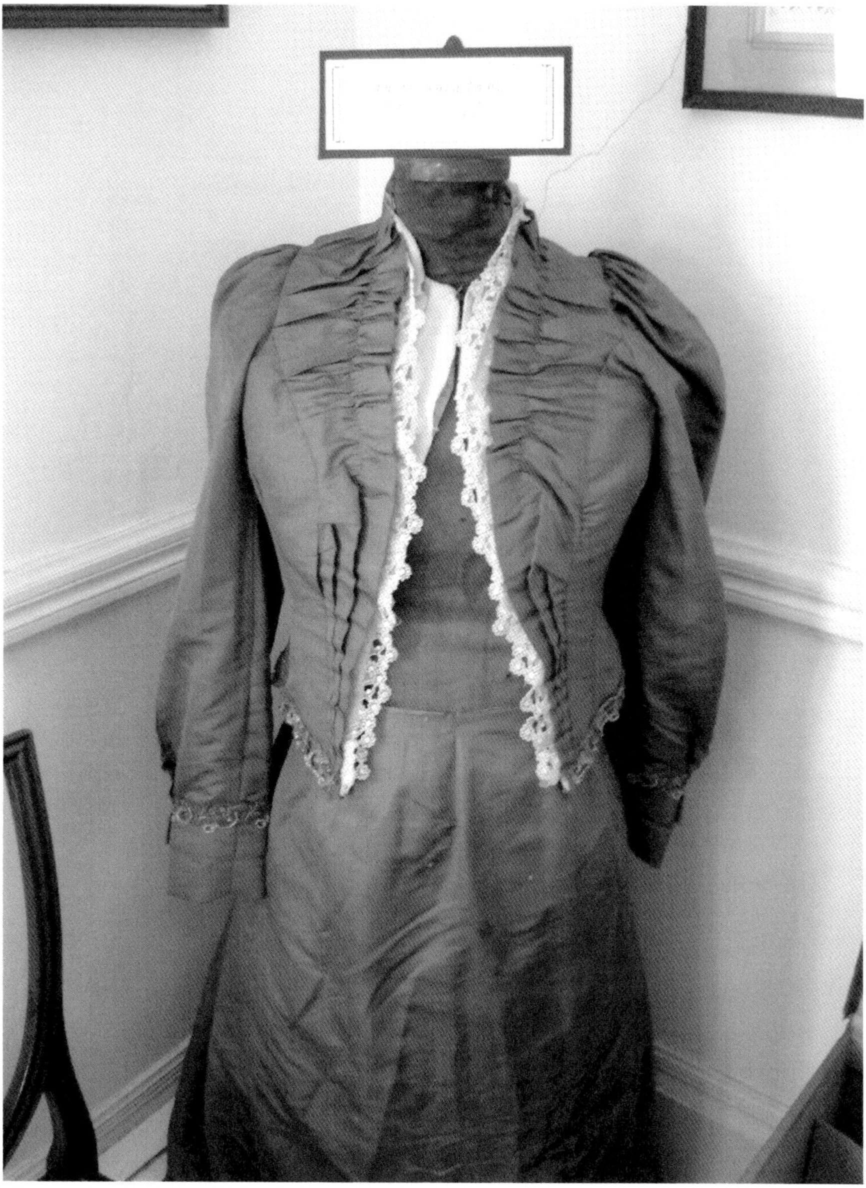

Dress circa 1890, once worn by Aunt Kate Poor. *From the collection of the Farmington Historical Society, photo by Elizabeth Buckingham.*

doe and was amazed when she didn't fall. A lot of other hunters told similar stories that season. They had her in their sights, but somehow she got away. They talked about her all winter, and the next season sportsmen were eager to find her again.

In 1896, the *Farmington Chronicle* reported on the experiences of John Shepard of Phillips, a crack shot who held a championship badge for marksmanship. Shepard was hunting in the same area where the doe had been seen the previous year when he met up with her. In his orchard, he had lain in wait between two boulders, and the deer came bounding into the clearing toward him. He waited until she got quite close, took deliberate aim and fired. He was sure the bullet had hit her, but the deer fled. He followed, expecting to find her down not far away. Soon he reached an open spot where he saw her. She hadn't fallen; in fact, she didn't appear to be suffering at all. She was standing on a knoll, calmly looking back at Shepard. He had a second easy shot at her, and he took it. Again he thought he hit her. Again, she turned and ran away. He followed, and the story repeated itself a third time. She paused to give him another try and then appeared to be

Deer hunters, circa 1900. *Photo courtesy of the Wilton Farm and Home Museum.*

impervious to the bullet. Shepard did not give up yet. He spent the rest of the day searching for the doe he was sure must have been hit.

Alive or dead, he never found her.

The experience plagued Shepard and, being a logical man, he concluded that the problem must be with his gun. When he got home, he tested it. He paced a distance twice that of his last shot and set up a board for a target. In twenty consecutive shots, he hit the board every time; sixteen times he was within four inches of the center.

Shepard was not superstitious, yet he came to a startling conclusion. His failure to shoot the deer was not his fault or the rifle's. According to the *Farmington Chronicle*, "He cannot account for it on any other grounds than that the deer bears a charmed life."

## Bolt of Lightning Strikes Kingfield

When lightning strikes, we tend to think of it as an act of God. So what does it mean when lightning strikes a worship service? Residents of Kingfield must have asked themselves this question after the bizarre events of a summer day in 1902.

On a Friday afternoon in August, Mrs. Barker attended the Holiness Camp Meeting in her hometown of Kingfield. Part social event, part religious ceremony, camp meetings were popular at the time. A dynamic traveling minister could often attract crowds who congregated under massive tents to hear the word of the Lord. Townspeople looked forward to seeing friends and neighbors to chat about the weather and crops. They expected to hear a forceful sermon from a man of the cloth who called upon them to change their evil ways.

The air hung heavy over Kingfield on this Friday afternoon when Mrs. Barker ventured out to hear the Reverend Truman's sermon. Barker was fifty-five years old, a respected member of the Baptist church and mother of four. By 1902, two of her children were grown and gone, while the two youngest still lived at home. That day she was without her husband George, a carpenter, who had gone to Madrid, but in the crowded tent she was surrounded by friends.

The storm began in the middle of the service and was as sudden as it was violent. Before anyone had time to react, the wind was whipping through the field, the rain was coming down in sheets, thunder was clapping continuously and lightning was flashing everywhere.

Then in the midst of the Holiness Camp Meeting, a bolt of lightning struck the tent. In a flash, several worshippers, including Reverend Truman's young daughter, were knocked unconscious by the shock. Mrs. Barker was struck worse than unconscious. The bolt of lightning that knocked out several people in the congregation had struck her dead.

The same afternoon, lightning hit the Kingfield Methodist Church as well. In other parts of Kingfield, the torrential rain wreaked havoc along with the lightning. Roads, culverts and bridges washed out. Two women narrowly escaped plunging into a raging stream with their team and carriage because they didn't know a bridge had been carried away. Grain crops around Kingfield had shown much promise that summer until they were ruined by one afternoon's torrential rains.

Damage from the summer storm of 1902 was sporadic. The Fryeburg area suffered a heavy downfall of hail an inch thick that destroyed all of its crops. Heavy rains between Rumford and Dixfield washed out the rail lines in several spots. Meanwhile, many localities in central Maine were not hit by severe weather at all that Friday afternoon. But for the community of Kingfield, and especially the Barker family, the storm made a mark that could never be undone.

## AN EARLY UFO IN FARMINGTON

In the winter of 1915, the *Franklin Journal* reported a "mysterious airship haunting Western Maine." Residents out late at night were spooked by the sound of humming overhead and a beam of light illuminating the ground. Herbert Parker saw the airship from West Farmington. He said he could plainly see the beam of light pierce the night sky as the machine dove in various directions "rising and falling and cutting big circles in the air." Parker watched until it finally disappeared, heading in the direction of New Sharon.

Later that same evening, John Higgins and his wife watched the airship for over an hour as it maneuvered over Clearwater Pond. Higgins claimed that just before it flew out of sight it was joined by a second one.

Just a dozen years after the Wright brothers' landmark flight from Kitty Hawk, the sight of any airship in the sky was worth noting. An unidentified object buzzing overhead under the cover of darkness, circling Clearwater Pond and diving over Farmington Falls was downright scary. Mainers were abuzz and came up with all kinds of theories to explain these strange sightings. A prevalent one centered on the wartime concern that much of Maine's railway system was controlled by British interests and was consequently susceptible to German attack. Across the Atlantic, the Great War was raging, and while America was still two years away from becoming officially involved, New Englanders were already feeling the threat.

But in retrospect, their concern doesn't seem plausible. The idea that German tactics would include attacking America with airplanes, still in experimental stages, seems preposterous. Western Maine was probably safe from the Germans, as it would be another four years before any airplane would fly across the Atlantic. Still, the newspaper reports that the rumor was taken seriously enough to "cause shivers of apprehension to chase up and down the backs of the Grand Trunk Railway managers."

Another rumor, circulated by the *Portland Press*, was that two aviators were hidden in the mountains of Oxford County, where they were secretly developing a new airplane. The press did not speculate that Wright brothers' protégé Harry Atwood was involved, but about that time the aeronautical pioneer disappeared from public view to move to an undisclosed location somewhere in the hills of New England. Three years earlier, Atwood had piloted the first plane to land in Maine. Maybe in 1915 Atwood and other early aviators were testing new designs alone in the darkness high above the lakes and mountains of western Maine. Yet to do this, they would have had to build a secret runway in their remote mountain hideout, not an easy feat in itself.

Whatever had been inhabiting the skies over western Maine disappeared into the night, and the mysterious airship could never be explained.

Chapter Six

# POLITICS, WAR AND SOCIETY

## The Thompson Indian War

During the War of 1812, residents feared that Indians, in league with the British, could strike at any minute. Rumors abounded that "savages" would make their way from Canada to infiltrate the mountain settlements of western Maine, scalping men, women and children and torching their homes and barns. Consequently, nervous residents were ready to spring into action at the slightest provocation.

Billy Thompson, a farmer in Avon, was an excitable man with a bad stutter. On a summer day in 1813, he was searching for lost cattle in the woods when something set him off. Whatever sound or sight scared Billy that day has been lost to history. But something alarmed him, and soon he was running and shouting, "Indians! Indians!"

Residents took Billy seriously. Without delay, they left their homes and fields to band together in some of the bigger, sturdier structures. Fifty years later a writer for the *Farmington Chronicle*, who called himself only "Senex," looked back on this overreaction with bemusement.

"Being without arms and ammunition with which to defend themselves," he wrote, "their congregating together would have only enabled the savages, had they really come, to have killed them with less trouble than to have gone from house to house to find their victims."

Even though no tangible sign of an Indian attack could be demonstrated, settlers in the Avon and Phillips area remained huddled together for days. The usual routine of tending farm animals and fields was suspended as families braced themselves as best they could for the dreaded Indians.

When the feeling of terror finally began to subside, Elijah Howland, Elijah Clark and James Thompson from Avon, as well as Mr. Hardy and Mr. Davenport from Phillips, decided it was time to go on a scouting party. Their search yielded no enemy or sign of enemy, but it did have one unforeseen and positive consequence: in their travels the men passed beyond Saddleback Mountain and saw the Rangeley Lakes for the first time. Near the area that is now Rangeley village, the explorers found something even more intriguing than the lake itself: great quantities of trout; enough, in fact, to fill a barrel.

As time went by and the Indian threat subsided, the residents of Avon and Phillips could actually look back on their phantom attack with humor. Over time, the incident came to be known as the Thompson Indian War.

## RUM AND ELECTIONS

Imagine a newly elected state representative hosting a party in the local park and serving liquor—free of charge—to the voting public to celebrate his victory. Imagine taxpayers outraged when the representatives refused to do this. Times have certainly changed in this respect since the early days of Farmington's history. Then it was the custom, according to historian Francis Gould Butler, "for the representatives to place a barrel of New England rum upon the Common, and invite friend and foe to partake." That was the custom, that is, until General William Gould was elected to the legislature in 1822.

Gould was one of the founding fathers of Farmington, arriving here from Dunstable, Massachusetts, in 1782. He evidently was not a big fan of drinking, although most of his fellow townspeople were. When Gould won the election, he refused to spring for the expected barrel of rum, and this upset those who were looking forward to the customary celebration. Townspeople stormed into the meetinghouse to make speeches and pass resolutions about what they considered unstatesmanlike conduct on Gould's part. Gould was not being cheap, however, and to prove his point he soon made a donation to benefit the school system. A barrel of New England rum cost twelve dollars, so he gave that sum to the town. Furthering children's education seemed more prudent than throwing a party, as far as Gould was concerned. He set a precedent, and the custom in which newly elected officials treated their constituents to liquor was never revived. Gould was a forerunner to the prohibition movement that had its beginnings in Farmington just a few years later.

Farmington Village, circa 1878. *From a mural in Franklin Savings Bank on Main Street, Farmington, painted by Melanie Farmer, 1989, photo by Elizabeth Buckingham.*

In 1829, the First Moral Temperance Society of Farmington was formed, led by John Allen, who probably knew a thing or two about the effects of liquor firsthand. "As a young man he was wild and reckless, fond of the excitement of rude frolics," his biographer notes. Allen very suddenly and dramatically changed his evil ways, however, after he found the Lord at a camp meeting, a salvation show in which a traveling preacher would endeavor to win souls for Christ. Allen was so moved by this experience that afterward he couldn't get enough of these kinds of gatherings. He attended camp meetings all over the country and became known as Camp Meeting John. He eventually became a preacher and, in his old age, served as a chaplain in the Maine House of Representatives in 1879 and 1881.

Twelve of Farmington's leading men composed the first Temperance Society, whose stated objective was "to do away, as far as practicable, the evil of intemperance." They pledged "to abstain from the use of intoxicating liquors except in case of absolute necessity when prescribed by a temperate physician as medicine." At one time in Farmington's history, public drinking was a part of the culture, but those days disappeared with leaders like Gould and Allen who took a stand against "the evil of intemperance."

## HEROES AND VILLAINS IN NINETEENTH-CENTURY POLITICS

Ballot controversies. Elections won and lost on technicalities. Enraged party members vehemently defending their candidate's right to office. A recap of the presidential election of 2000? Yes. But these scenarios also describe Maine's turbulent election of 1879. Between the vote in September of that year and the inauguration of candidates in January 1880, conflict over election returns raged in every county in the state. Farmington was one of many towns hit by the controversy when state officials ruled that the election of the area's state representative did not count because of voting irregularities.

According to reports in the *Franklin Chronicle* and *Boston Journal*, Maine's election controversy of 1879 had its beginnings in a conspiracy that was hatched months before unsuspecting voters went to the polls. The culprits in this underhanded plan were Fusionists, members of the Democratic and Greenback Parties who had fused in an effort to beat the Republicans. At a meeting in Calais, these politicians pledged to send their candidates to the legislature in 1880 even if they had to cheat to do so. The goal of these conspirators was not just to see their party represented within the state but to secure Maine's electoral vote for the Democratic presidential candidate in the subsequent national election.

The *Franklin Chronicle* reported that one of the first plans implemented by the conspirators, evidently with the help of the secretary of state and state printer, was to send blank ballots to some towns that were likely to vote Republican. Evidently this was viewed as no more than an honest mistake at the time, and the vast majority of Maine citizens were oblivious to any plot.

In Farmington, Louis Voter challenged incumbent Cyrus Thomas for the position of state representative. Thomas was a Republican from West Farmington. Not much is known about him, but he was no doubt younger than his challenger. Voter was seventy-five years old when he decided to run for state representative on the Democratic ticket. A Mason, he lived in the village, where he was active in town affairs, serving as selectman for two years and treasurer for one.

Voting seemed routine that election day, with the selectmen, all of them Democrats, overseeing the procedure in Farmington. In fact, it wasn't until a couple of months later that the general public began to smell a rat. Four candidates had run for governor and no gubernatorial candidate won a majority, so statute called for the election to be decided by the state legislature. Suddenly, the outcome of the legislative races took on added importance and fell under increased scrutiny. Initial counts showed the Republicans winning a majority in the legislature, but it was the responsibility of the governor and his appointed council to confirm or reject these election results. This is when Democratic Governor Alonzo Garcelon and his council voided the election of a dozen Republican legislators on technical grounds. Soon accusations were flying thick and fast and charges of conspiracy, fraud and open defiance of the Constitution reached the highest levels of state government. This series of events led to "a devil of a time" as Maine citizens approached Inauguration Day with no agreement about whom to inaugurate.

The Fusion Party seemed to be itching for a fight. In late December, the *Farmington Chronicle* reported that the Fusionist representative-elect from Oxford had received a letter from his party's leaders urging him to be prepared for violent controversy over his inauguration. Come "with ten good men" they told him, to help defend himself against Republican opposition. Their expenses would be paid.

On New Year's Day, Governor Garcelon put the statehouse under armed guard while a political meeting in Farmington attracted one of the largest crowds ever assembled in the history of the town. Many citizens, Republicans, Democrats and Greenbacks alike, denounced Garcelon's tactics. Prominent businessman Reuben Cutler announced that even though he was a lifelong Democrat, he did not condone the actions of his party in Augusta. Meetings in surrounding communities echoed the same sentiments. A resolve out of Phillips stated, "While we still hope some peaceful solution to the difficulty may be found…we do not propose to be governed by men who were never elected."

One of those men "never elected" was Voter, who had run for state representative in the district that included both Farmington and Perkins Plantation. He had lost in Farmington by thirty-six votes and won Perkins Plantation by only one vote. However, Garcelon's council in Augusta had thrown out the Farmington results on technicalities, declaring Democrat Voter the winner. In the time between September's election and January's showdown, Voter had remained quiet about his intentions regarding this upset victory. On Monday, January 5, legislators-elect began showing up in Augusta. Some were Republicans, some Fusionists. Some had been elected fairly, some had won their district's vote only to see the results overturned and others had been "appointed" by Garcelon. Voter was not among them. He remained home and kept his opinions to himself.

Then, on Monday night, Voter answered a knock on his door to find Phillips lawyer Prince Albert Sawyer impatiently waiting on the other side. Maine's secretary of state, P.A. Sawyer, wanted to whisk Voter away to Augusta for the inauguration. Sawyer had traveled secretly to Farmington under cover of night to personally persuade the elderly Mason to take his seat in the legislature.

Sawyer was an ambitious man, and some might say a restless and reckless one. He had grown up in Phillips and moved to Illinois at age sixteen, where he taught school and within a year became a principal, despite his lack of even a high school education. At twenty years old, he returned to Maine and married Elvira Oakes in Temple. Becoming a principal was relatively easy in those days, and so was becoming a lawyer. Sawyer studied law, passed the bar exam within a matter of months and became a lawyer. Sawyer then returned to Illinois, this time with a new wife and a new profession. However, when he was twenty-six, the death of his sister in Phillips drew him back there to care for his aging parents.

In 1879, still only thirty-three, Sawyer became deputy secretary of state during Garcelon's administration. He was swept up in the Fusionists' decision to oust the Republicans by any means necessary and became an accomplice to Garcelon's attempt to tamper with election results by "counting out" legitimate Republican wins on technicalities.

By surprising Voter in the middle of the night, Sawyer had forced his hand, and now Voter had to decide. Would he take the position of power, knowing that he had been elected unfairly? Since Sawyer was from Franklin County, Voter probably knew him personally, and Sawyer was persistent. He told Voter that even if the Farmington candidate's own election had been unconstitutional, it was right to declare himself the winner, that in order to beat the Republicans the end justified the means. He said that if Voter stayed away it would be the heaviest blow the state's Fusionist Party had ever received. He proposed to take the seventy-five-year-old by open sleigh to Augusta that very night, despite the January cold.

Voter declined. He had not been fairly elected, he told Sawyer.

"He has labored too long and too hard in this community," observed the *Farmington Chronicle* in regard to Voter, "to build up a character that has been marked from youth to age by industry, honesty, and integrity, to allow it now to be blackened and smirched by any contact with this infamy."

Sawyer returned to Augusta alone that same night. Thanks to Voter and five other illegally elected Fusionist candidates who refused to get caught up in the fray, the party could not form a quorum. This meant that the runoff gubernatorial election could not be held. Garcelon's term expired with no legal governor being sworn in to take his place.

In the days that followed, the militia kept a fragile order in Augusta as state supreme court justices deliberated over the election results, election rules and the law. Much as their successors in the election of 2000, these supreme court justices were asked to bring order and reason to chaos. On January 17, the state supreme court reinstated the Republican legislators whose elections had been thrown out by Fusionists on technical grounds. Republican Daniel Davis was inaugurated governor later that same day.

Order slowly returned to Augusta in the days that followed, although some of the more vehement Fusionists refused to abandon their sinking ship. Some of the ousted legislators banned together to hold their own legislative session. Since they were no longer welcome in the statehouse, they convened in the street. Among the most resistant Fusion leaders was Prince Sawyer, who had, amidst the chaos, been elected secretary of state. After Davis was inaugurated, Sawyer refused to give up the keys to the statehouse safe. When the safe was opened by force, officials found the state seal missing, along with legislative and county election returns.

A week after the Republicans had been restored to power, rumors were still in the air that Fusion leaders were attempting to occupy the statehouse. Fear was heightened when the telegraph wire to the capitol was cut in the night. Three companies of infantry were called out to surround the building, which was enough to deter the Fusionists, if an overthrow had actually been in the works. On January 28, the supreme court decided against the Fusionists' appeal, which seemed to be the death knell for the already weakened revolt. The headline in the next day's *Farmington Chronicle* announced, "The Farce is Over!" "When this impartial record shall have been written of the conspiracy that has nearly turned our heretofore orderly State into a scene of anarchy, and disgraced our name, it will be one of the darkest pages ever penned in American history," *Farmington Chronicle* editor Charles W. Keyes observed.

The missing state seal is now the stuff of legend from one of Maine's "darkest pages." Some say Prince Sawyer threw the seal in the Kennebec River, and the incriminating election returns with it. Others joke that Phillips actually became the capital of Maine for few days. They claim to know that the state seal was hiding there under Prince Sawyer's bed.

Sawyer was never charged with a crime or disbarred for his part in the chaos of that January, and he returned to Phillips to once again devote himself fully to the practice of law. He eventually became a member of the party he had plotted and schemed so hard to overthrow. At forty-three, he and his family again picked up roots and moved to the Midwest, this time settling in Sioux City, Iowa. Sawyer quickly became involved in Iowa politics and was elected to the Iowa General Assembly a few years later—not as a Democrat, but as a Republican.

Probably no one in Iowa knew of his part in Maine's "scene of anarchy," and perhaps he took to his grave the secret whereabouts of the Maine state seal.

## COLUMBUS DAY IN THE NINETEENTH CENTURY

It's easy to pinpoint the first time the American flag flew from atop a public school in Farmington and the first time the Pledge of Allegiance was ever recited here. In Farmington and across the country, these hallmarks of patriotism can trace their origins to Columbus Day in 1892. While pledging allegiance to the flag has become a part of most children's school day, the origins of these traditions are as full of contradictions and surprises as America itself.

The year 1892 marked the 400th anniversary of Christopher Columbus's voyage to the New World, and Americans celebrated with demonstrations of national pride and patriotism. Francis Bellamy fell in line with the nation's sentiments when he planned a school program on behalf of the National Education Association. The program included a flag raising ceremony and something he wrote called a Pledge of Allegiance, which was published in a popular magazine called *Youth's Companion* just a few weeks before the big event.

Schools across the country embraced the ideas, and it is estimated that on that Columbus Day 1892 more than twelve million schoolchildren recited this pledge for the first time. Farmington students were very much a part of this phenomenon, and primary students here also witnessed the beginnings of another tradition. On the morning of Columbus Day, they watched as a new American flag was raised above their school building. The use of flags in public schools was also the result of a promotion by *Youth's Companion* magazine, which had sold some twenty-six thousand flags to American schools between 1888 and 1892.

After the flag raising, schoolchildren of all ages joined Wheeler's Band for a high-stepping parade that marched its way around downtown and ended at the Music Hall (now Reny's Department Store) on Broadway.

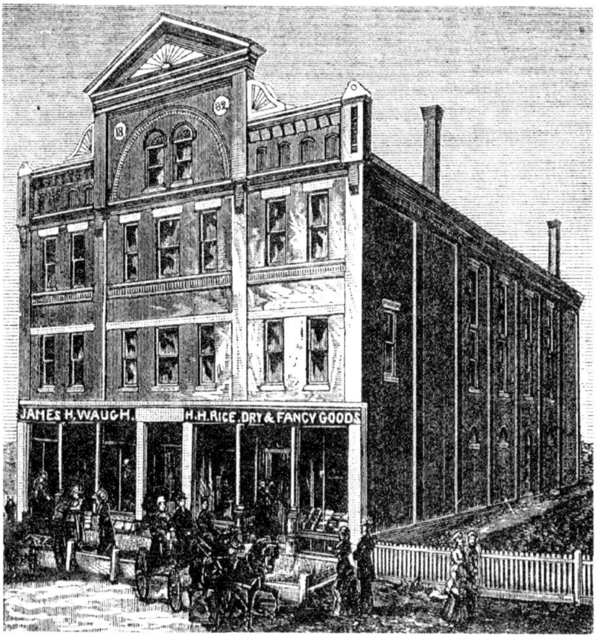


The Music Hall building on Broadway, now Reny's Department Store. *Drawing courtesy of the Farmington Historical Society.*

Young parade participants entered the hall in practiced military formation and spectators followed.

The program drew an astonishing eight hundred spectators who watched as students rose, extended their right arms stiffly toward the stars and stripes and recited this new pledge. As townspeople stood crowded into the hall decorated with "bunting, flags and pictures of prominent military commanders" and listened to the words "I pledge allegiance…" they couldn't know that they were witnessing the beginnings of a tradition. They also didn't know that Bellamy, the author of the pledge, was a committed socialist, or that he had wanted to include the word "equality" in his pledge but had refrained, lamenting that it would be "too many thousands of years off in realization." They didn't know that fifty years later, in a world war, the straight-arm salute would become the symbol of a tyrant named Adolph Hitler. They didn't know that the words "under God" would be added to what had been written as an entirely secular pledge. They couldn't see the future, and yet the newspaper reporter at the time heralded the event as "an occasion never to be forgotten."

## COMPANY K MARCHES AWAY

In 1915, a German submarine attacked and sunk a passenger ship that was sailing from New York City to England, leaving 1,200 people dead. The sinking of the *Lusitania* angered Americans, and bitterness against Germany grew.

In April 1917, the United States officially entered what would later be known as World War I and the men of Farmington's Company K faced daily reminders that their lives would soon be in upheaval. Some of these came in odd ways. "The Largest Days in History are Ahead of Us" proclaimed an ad from Hardy's Pharmacy in the *Franklin Chronicle*. The ad urged customers to purchase the larger packages of A.D.S. Remedies because "it is economy to save."

"Again has our gallant Company K, Assembled together to march away," noted an ad for Norton's Candy Store. The country will need men who can serve "scientifically," which is the same way the store produces its ice cream, the ad explained.

Company K, October 1916, leaving for the Mexican border. *Photo courtesy of the Farmington Historical Society.*

War bonds were selling with 4 percent interest. "REAL MEN—with real blood in their veins" were wanted for the National Guard, and on Patriot's Day the men of Company K assembled on Broadway to listen to an address by Judge J.H. Thompson. "The Kaiser in his inhuman fashion has made war on this peace loving people," he told the crowd. As the young men in Company K listened, Thompson warned ominously of the days ahead. "We are coming fast to realize that our life, liberty and pursuit of happiness can only be preserved by shedding the blood of the youth freely on the land and sea."

A week later Company K marched to the train station on Front Street as Wheeler's Band played patriotic music and a crowd of well-wishers turned out to cheer them on. "They certainly made a fine and imposing appearance as they left town," noted the local newspaper editor. This was the last time some of the members of Company K would ever see their loved ones, their hometown or the mountains of western Maine. The blood of many would indeed be spilled on land and sea, and some of them—including Charles Foote, Dan Gould and Thaddeus Roderick—would not survive to return home.

## Chapter Seven

# PROFILES

## The Last Native American

The Farmington area's last Native American was a mythical figure to most residents, and stories of his ways and wanderings were handed down from generation to generation. Pealpole Coweasme was an interesting blend of cultures. Clad in Indian blankets, moccasins and silver jewelry, he looked nothing like his white neighbors, but dressed the part of a member of the Androscoggin tribe. His wife Hannah Susup was a member of the Noridgewok. His religion was Catholic but much of his lifestyle was similar to that of his Protestant neighbors. He farmed; he lived in a frame house; he sent his son to school.

Pealpole had served in the Revolutionary War and earned the title captain. After marrying Hannah, he lived with her people until moving to the Farmington Falls area, probably sometime in the late 1770s. Pealpole and his family were the only Native Americans living there when Englishmen first explored the area. From Farmington Falls, the family moved to Read-Town (now the town of Strong), where he was given one hundred acres of land with frontage along the Sandy River (no doubt as payment for his service in the Revolutionary War) and also acquired another one hundred acres east of the Sandy.

Although his appearance and accent set him apart, he had assimilated many of the white settlers' ways. The stereotype of the Indian wigwam and hunting grounds did not apply to Pealpole. After moving to Readstown, he became only the second settler in the area to build a frame house. He farmed his land as his white neighbors did. He hunted with a rifle, and legend has it

Pealpole and friend spear fish as Joseph North surveys the Sandy River Lower Township (soon to become Farmington), 1780. Artist's depiction. *From a mural by Rober Deering, 1939, in the law office of Frank M. Underkuffler, photo by Elizabeth Buckingham.*

he made his own bullets from secret lead deposits in Day Mountain. Whether he encountered any discrimination, Pealpole was a part of the Sandy River Valley community. When his daughters, Molly Susup and Molly Pealpole, married Indians from other parts of the state, their vows were recorded in town records like any other citizen's. Pealpole was illiterate, but he sent his son Joseph to Supply Belcher's neighborhood school.

One of the things that made Pealpole seem so exotic to his neighbors in Farmington and Strong was not his Indian ways at all, but his religion. Pealpole was a devout Catholic; his tribe or family had no doubt been converted by French Canadian fur traders or missionaries. Every year he traveled to Canada to make offerings to his church and receive benediction. The lack of a nearby priest often made life difficult because it was so important to him that his children receive the blessings of the church. When his son Iganoose died, Pealpole preserved the body with smoke and then transported it to Canada for a Catholic burial.

He took his youngest daughter, Hannah, on an arduous journey to the Penobscot, where he counted on finding a priest to perform the all-important baptismal ceremony. No priest was found, however, and Pealpole returned home with Hannah unbaptized. Shortly after, the young girl fell sick and died. Pealpole buried his little girl on a hill in Strong beneath a cedar tree. He bent the tree over and tied it down to create an arch over her grave. The loss was hard for Pealpole to bear, and he agonized over the fact that his daughter had never been baptized. Her death, he felt, was a curse from God for not having a priest's blessing on her soul. This tragedy may have led to his decision to leave the area.

In 1799, Pealpole sought the help of his friend Supply Belcher in petitioning the Massachusetts General Assembly to allow him to sell his granted land. In the petition (no doubt ghostwritten by Belcher), Pealpole explained that he had two reasons for desiring to move away. One was that his code of hospitality was draining his resources. He stated that "as there is not any other Indian family living near, I have so many visiting Indians, it keepeth me excessive Poor." By Pealpole's code of ethics, it would have been impossible to deny any of these travelers food or shelter. He was more willing to move than he was to turn away guests. Also, Pealpole was frustrated with being in the minority. Interestingly enough, this minority identity seemed to come more from being a Catholic than from being an Indian: "As my kindred live in Kanada, I wish to remove thither," he said, "not only that I may enjoy my friends, but that Religion which I was taught to observe."

Pealpole sold his parcel of land east of the Sandy River to Nathaniel Thompson from Bristol for $350. Thompson also wanted Pealpole's second lot with river frontage, but this land, which had been given to him by the Massachusetts legislature, was not easy to dispose of. Pealpole needed special permission from the State of Massachusetts before this lot could change hands. With the help of his friends William Read (founder of Strong) and Belcher, he devised a plan. He received from Thompson an additional $400 for the second lot. At the same time, he gave Read and Belcher power of attorney to draw up the petition to the Massachusetts General Assembly. The paperwork trail was a slow one, and the assembly did not actually consider the petition and give its official authorization until February 1801. Thompson did not officially become the owner of the lot until the deed was filed with Kennebec County in September 1802.

By then, Franklin County's most famous Native American was long gone. No doubt he was living in French Quebec, where he had found his own kind under the paternalism of the Roman Catholic Church. For generations to come, Farmington residents told tales of the only Native American they had ever known in these parts, the only link they had ever had to a more mysterious, mystical past.

## A Lifetime of Changes in Strong

Julia Eastman was born in Strong around 1800, at about the time the town was incorporated. Her world was small by our standards. A trip to Farmington was a journey she made only a few times a year. More bustling, populated cities like Lewiston, Portland or Boston were simply beyond the scope of her experience. But while her world consisted of the people and landscape within the boundaries of Strong, during her lifetime she witnessed almost a century of change in her mountain community.

When Julia was born, residents in her community were enjoying their newfound status as citizens of a town officially incorporated in the territory of Maine, state of Massachusetts. Incorporation was important to the development of communities in the wilderness, as it enabled residents to collect taxes, make improvements to roads and bridges, erect meetinghouses and generally make their communities more attractive to prospective settlers. More demand for property within a town meant higher land values and landowners were naturally eager to see their property values increase.

Until shortly before Julia was born, the community had been called Readstown. However, early settlers, mindful of the way politics and egos worked in Boston, took it upon themselves to request a new town name when they sought incorporation. They decided upon Strong, feeling that

A hooked rug by Julia Eastmann Stubbs, recently displayed in a folk art collection at the Maine State Museum. *Photo courtesy of the Maine State Museum.*

Massachusetts Governor Caleb Strong might be partial to the name and feel obliged to sign the town's incorporation papers. And so the town that Julia was born into was no longer called Readstown, but had taken on the new name of Strong. Although Strong was an incorporated town, life there was still very much like life in the wilderness: the handful of residents were isolated by mountainous terrain and severe winters. But when Julia was a teenager, the outside world drew a little closer when Strong first got a mail route. Now a letter from a relative in Boston, a newspaper from Portland or a magazine from New York City could arrive on a regular basis.

Even as a young woman, Julia cut a striking figure. She was tall and self-assured and she caught the attention of Philip Stubbs, a young lawyer practicing in Strong. When Julia was in her twenties, she married Philip. The wedding did not take place in a church because no church had yet been built in Strong. A year after her wedding, in 1835, the Methodist church was the first church erected in the village. By this time, the village also included a sawmill for lumber, a gristmill for flour and a tannery for leather.

Julia and Philip might have settled in town since Philip most likely had an office in town. However, they probably owned property south of the village because Stubbs Mountain is no doubt named for them. Julia and Philip had a son, whom they named Philip, who became a lawyer as well. In addition to practicing law, the Stubbs family also established a mill north of town on the Valley Brook. In Julia's later years, more changes came to her small community. She lived to see the railroad connect Strong to the rest of New England in ways she couldn't have imagined as a child. Now a round trip to Farmington or even Lewiston was possible to do in a day. Industry grew because businesses now had a more efficient way to ship their products out of Strong and into bigger markets. Forster Manufacturing and Starbird Lumber established themselves in Strong to take advantage of the successful logging operations in the area. Along with business came more outside visitors and a large impressive hotel.

Julia died in 1894, having lived nearly a century in the village of Strong. She had been born into a pioneer community cut off from urban areas by distances that seemed nearly insurmountable. By the time she died, her community had become connected to the greater world of commerce in ways those early pioneers had dimly hoped for but could have barely imagined.

## FARMINGTON'S MOTHER

When Eliza Rogers first came to Farmington in 1826, the area had been settled for less than fifty years. Compared to Newburyport, Massachusetts, her new home was still very much a frontier town, and no doubt this gave her misgivings. Back at Andover Seminary, her husband had been moved to join the Maine ministry. In fact, he had told the secretary of the Missionary Society that "if you have any place in Maine so destitute and unattractive that no one else will go, send me." And that is how Eliza arrived in Farmington with her husband Isaac.

She found a village without a church where her fellow Congregational parishioners had to make do with sharing the meetinghouse with other denominations, often organizing services at schools or private homes instead. When Eliza arrived, Maine had only been a state for five years and Franklin was yet to be a county. The town, still smarting from the effects of the War of 1812, had a sluggish economy and no newspaper. A disease called cold fever had ravaged the population, and a migration called Ohio fever had further depleted it. Despite these drawbacks, or maybe because of them, Eliza and Isaac arrived in Farmington in their one-horse chaise determined to put down roots and become a part of the community.

Eliza probably didn't know then that she would remain childless her entire life. As the years went by and no children were born to them, the couple gave their attention instead to the young people of their church and Greater Farmington. Eliza became known as "Mother Rogers" in recognition of her maternal instincts toward the community's children. She was even president of the Mother's Association, an early women's group. She led the group in prayer and gave advice and support to young mothers.

Childless and active in community organizations, Eliza's lifestyle was in many ways closer to today's women than to her contemporaries. Although she played hostess to many travelers, she was not known for her housekeeping and instead spent her time in church work along with her husband. She devoted herself to the church's missionary society. In the early

Reverend Isaac Rogers, husband of Eliza, circa 1858. *Photo courtesy of the Farmington Historical Society.*

years, Farmington itself had been on the receiving end of missionary funds, but as time went on the village began to thrive and church members were not so needy. They were even able to spare a little for struggling communities in more remote locations, and Eliza was a major fundraiser for this cause.

In some ways Eliza was very much a product of puritanical New England. In her day, some very strict church members considered dancing to be the work of the devil, and Eliza herself frowned upon dancing at church social events. At one party, Eliza was chatting with her friends in the parlor when she noticed that all the young people were missing. Suspicious, she left with the excuse of warming her feet at the cook stove. In the kitchen she found the teenagers in an impromptu dance, but they quickly scattered when Mother Rogers entered the room. While she frowned on dancing, she did not always censor the frivolous. At a sewing circle once, she delighted the young girl beside her by retelling the plot of a romance novel she had recently read. While they hemmed a sheet together, Mother Rogers chatted merrily about handsome heroes and beautiful heroines and obstacles in the face of passion. In fact, Eliza was an unapologetic fan of romance novels, despite the murmurs of those who thought a minister's wife should not read such material.

By 1867, Eliza had lived in Farmington for forty-two years. In that time her parishioners had acquired a church of their own and the town had acquired a newspaper. Franklin had become a county and Farmington had its own shopping district and bank. Train travel and the telegraph had brought the outside world closer. As she lay on her deathbed, she was surrounded by townspeople who had come to feel like family to her. "How is your condition?" asked one of her visitors.

"I do not know," she replied. "I have never been dying before."

## FROM CIVIL WAR VETERAN TO PEDDLER

Anyone entering the New York Stock Exchange on Broad Street in 1891 might have seen an armless man with a full blond beard selling pencils and pocketknives from a portable tray. He was Farmington native Charles Perham, whose life had taken some unpredictable turns.

Perham had been a teenager when he joined the army in 1864. His brother Silas had already been fighting with the Twenty-third Infantry for two years, but when Charles joined, Silas moved to the Fourth Maine Battery to be with his brother. The boys joined Grant's army in the middle of the nine-month siege of Petersburg, Virginia. They were encamped near Petersburg through the winter, and in the spring, after a general assault on

A company of Union infantry, Virginia, 1863. *From a photo of an unidentified company painted by Farmington artist C.R. Tyler, courtesy of the Farmington Historical Society.*

the Confederate lines, the Union army finally broke through and Petersburg fell in April. A week later Lee surrendered, and the efforts of the Fourth Maine Battery were no longer needed. During its years of service in the Civil War, six of the company's soldiers had died in battle. Worse yet, twenty-two had died of disease while living in the squalor of the Union camps.

Charles must have considered himself lucky that he and his brother had escaped injury and returned to Farmington healthy and unhurt. Tall and strong, he went to work as a blacksmith while his brother established a livery stable. A couple years after returning home, local veterans hosted a reunion. Having been in the artillery, Charles was chosen to join the squad to fire a cannon salute to the Union forces. As he was ramming home a charge, a premature explosion erupted, hurling Charles to the ground. When the smoke cleared, his fellow veterans found him still alive but terribly mangled. His face and body were badly burnt; his right arm had been torn off at the shoulder, his left shattered below the elbow. Charles had suffered an accident far more terrible than anything he had experienced in the midst of war and the repercussions were far worse than any battle fatigue he had known.

His predictable life as a blacksmith in a New England village was changed forever. After months of recovery, he found himself well again but had to face a future with no arms. He couldn't make a living as a blacksmith anymore

Abigail Hodgkins Knowlton, wife of Selden, mother of eight children; this photo was taken in 1898. *Photo courtesy of the Farmington Historical Society.*

but found he could use what remained of his left arm to carry light items. No doubt distraught about his condition, he left his brother Silas and his home in Farmington to become a peddler. He wandered out to California, where he sold his wares on a ferry between Oakland and San Francisco. Later he drifted eastward again, eventually resting in New York City, where he frequented Broad Street, eking out a living selling trinkets to stock brokers. By then the Civil War veteran was forty-five years old and his wandering days were nearing an end.

Two years later, he was back in Farmington, probably returning to seek care from his brother, who still ran the village livery stable. Here on a day in June 1893, he died at the age of forty-seven, and his final resting place was not a Civil War battlefield or a New York City pauper's grave but the Riverside Cemetery in his own hometown.

## Monument to a Teacher

In the Strong Cemetery stands a monument erected to the memory of Sara May "by loving pupils of the May School." The ten-foot-high white marble marker is as stately now as the day it was placed over her grave site, and the engraving is as easy to read as the day her former pupil, John Soule, first carved the words of tribute.

Sara was born in Strong in 1835 to a family who stressed education. She and her sister Julia were good students, and Sara went on to train as a teacher at Mount Holyoke Seminary. She taught in public schools in Strong and Winthrop and then headed west to join her sister in Kentucky. But Sara's health was poor, and after a few years the sisters returned to Maine. When Sara felt well enough again, the sisters decided to open a private school of their own in Farmington. In 1868, they established the May School for Girls, offering instruction in Latin, French and high mathematics.

"She seemed to be possessed of a happy faculty of gaining the love of her pupils and interesting them in everything good, whether of a literary, moral, or religious character," recalled one of Sara's pupils years later. The women's institution was immediately successful. With no public high school in town, it filled a need for a college preparatory curriculum, and soon many families wanted to send their sons as well as daughters. The sisters expanded and renamed their school the Wendell Institute. It remained small; only the wealthier families could afford to educate their children beyond eighth grade. Forty-five students graduated from the school during its thirteen-year existence in Farmington. Many alumni went on to prestigious colleges such as Vassar, Wellesley, Bowdoin and Bates.

In 1877, the town of Farmington established a public high school and the May sisters' private school began to lose patrons. In 1881, the sisters moved their institution to their hometown of Strong. Seven years later, Sara died at the age of fifty-three. She was buried in the Strong Cemetery, initially beneath a modest granite marker. But by then, some of her students had returned to Farmington to raise families and pursue careers. Among them were attorneys Arthur Belcher and Elmer Richards. In 1892, they decided to honor their former teacher with a monument to her efforts and sent out a fundraising letter.

"From all over the country came the responses with contributions larger or smaller," remembered an organizer, "and almost always an added spontaneous word of love for 'Miss Sara.'"

## Chapter Eight

# NATURE

### Varnum Pond's Giant Trout

More than a century ago, Timothy Woodward was walking along the shore of Varnum Pond in Wilton when he came upon the biggest trout he'd ever seen. Because it was dead and beached, Woodward was able to get a good look and still could hardly believe his eyes. The trout was about three feet long and must have weighed nearly forty pounds. Probably the tough old fish had finally died from old age, but as Woodward studied the carcass he could tell it had put up its share of fights. Parts of old broken hooks protruded from its mouth, along with one hook still whole, a line still attached. Woodward never forgot the mammoth fish he discovered that day. The story was retold in the *Farmington Chronicle* in 1867, which is how it comes to us today.

In the late 1700s and early 1800s, early settlers in western Maine valued trout as a tasty source of meat, especially when times got rough. In 1816, an unseasonably cold summer led to crop failure. Without the usual harvests of wheat and corn, trout became crucial to the survival of struggling families. While ten pounds is considered a good-sized trout today, tales of fifteen-, twenty- or twenty-five-pound trout were common in the 1800s. Writer John Willard, a Wilton resident, claimed that in 1840 he could buy a sixteen-pounder for one dollar. However, prices increased rapidly after that and, twenty years later, local fishermen could sell the trout for a dollar a pound. With such inflated prices, the fish became a "cash crop." Locals needed the money far more than they needed the trout dinner. Consequently, they fished with the intention of selling their catch, and local lake trout most often would find their way to the tables of exclusive Boston restaurants and palatial private homes.

## NEW VINEYARD MOUNTAINS' "TREACHEROUS" WOLVES

Anyone who heard the sound felt a jolt of fear. It was a "weird howling" such as to make their hair stand on end. In 1899, residents in the New Vineyard Mountains feared the return of the wolves. They had been prevalent in western Maine until settlement by farmers who had wiped out the animals as quickly as possible. Legend has it that the last wolf was slaughtered near Norton Mountain sometime in the late 1800s. Residents of the area were alarmed to hear the howling of a wolf in the winter of 1899. A correspondent to the *Lewiston Evening Journal* called the wolf "the most cruel and treacherous of all North American beasts" and boasted that "if much more of this night howling is heard there will be a battle in the woods some fine day."

Wolves were perceived to be a threat to one of rural Maine's most important sources of meat. "The residents of that section are pretty good deer hunters and don't want to see their favorite animal driven away," observed the correspondent. But the fear and hatred that wolves aroused went even deeper than that. Maine wildlife biologist Deb Davidson observed in 2004 that historically, the "blood curdling" howl itself has been enough to strike fear in people's hearts. And then there are the children's stories: "Little Red Riding Hood," "The Three Pigs," "Peter and the Wolf." In all of them, the wolf is a beast to be feared.

In reality, wolves are no more aggressive than other animals in the wild. "Most of the time they run from you," said Davidson. "You don't see a wolf in the woods because they are gone. They see you first." In fact, she said, in the lower forty-eight states there has never been a fatal attack on a human by a wolf. "Wolves don't run the deer population down," Davidson added. Instead, they thin out the weak and sick ones.

## RANGELEY'S "VICIOUS" BEARS

In January 1914, Franklin County residents feared that the native black bears were out to get them. In the middle of winter, the local newspaper reported rumors that in the Rangeley area, bears were "so thick that they hunted in packs like wolves." Today, few would give credence to such a story.

"Absolutely contrary to bear nature," observed University of Maine at Farmington biology professor Ron Butler in 2005. "Most bears are denned up in January."

Hand-loomed blanket owned by Lydia Titcomb, daughter of Elizabeth and Stephen Titcomb. *From the collection of the Farmington Historical Society, photo by Elizabeth Buckingham.*

Fairgrounds in Farmington, September 1909. *Photo courtesy of the Farmington Historical Society.*

Jennifer Vashon of the Maine Department of Inland Fisheries and Wildlife agreed. Bears hibernate in winter and they just don't run in packs. In fact, the wildlife biologist said, "You don't see bears interacting, except in family groups and during breeding season."

Yet a century ago, tales were told of how area residents Jim Mathieson and Jim Stewart were chased by "these vicious and ferocious beasts." According to people who study bears today, the animals have historically been victims of bad publicity. We no longer consider bears to be "vicious and ferocious."

"Sounds to me like the popular mythology that was prevalent," said Butler. Vashon pointed out that childhood fables like Goldilocks influenced people's image of bears. "Fear of predators took a long time to go away," she observed.

As the 1914 story goes, Steward and Mathieson became alarmed when they saw several bears in the woods near Oquossoc. Stewart shot at one but didn't kill it. His story intrigued some of the local hunters, including G.W. Fanjoy, who put together a group of hunters and a bear dog to travel to Oquossoc to see for themselves. When the hunting party got to the forest around Oquossoc, the group split in two. Fanjoy took the dog and followed bear prints until, suddenly, the bear they had been tracking rose up from behind a dead tree. According to the newspaper report, she "drew back her lips in angry snarl and just dared them to come on." Fanjoy quickly raised his gun and fired, killing the bear instantly. Getting a glimpse of another one hiding behind some brush, he quickly shot that one too.

"Negative things happen when a bear feels cornered, or you come between a mother and cubs," said Vashon. This is what had happened to Fanjoy. After the animals were dead, he discovered he had killed a very thin, and already wounded, mother bear, probably the one Stewart had shot earlier in the season. Lying dead now beside her was her ten-month-old cub.

## Chapter Nine

# TRAGEDY AND PERSEVERANCE

### The Watery Grave

Like any family on vacation, the Thomases expected to have a wonderful time. In 1892, when they decided to spend a couple of Indian summer weeks on Loon Lake near Rangeley, they didn't imagine tragedy would strike. Today we might say they should have seen it coming, but in their day people did not think of safety precautions the way we do.

Apparently, no one in the Thomas family knew how to swim, yet they planned their vacation around water activities, fishing and boating the dozen or so lakes near Forest Camps. What is worse, their guide didn't seem to know how to swim either. No one could even keep their head above water, and yet they went out on the lakes every day without any sort of flotation devices in their boat.

Whether they feared the water they were so unprepared for, we don't know, but the Thomas family was having a wonderful time in the early part of their stay. They slept well on spring beds, dined well on roast pork and fried trout and enjoyed a striking view of Loon Lake and Kennebago West Mountain. Twenty-year-old Marcia Thomas loved to draw the mountains, the pine trees and the water. The entire family enjoyed catching fish.

There was a hint of fall in the air when Mr. and Mrs. Thomas and their three daughters set out Friday morning in early September for another day of fishing. Their guide, Marsh Carlton, took them to Greeley Pond, where he had a spot in mind on the far side. Not everybody could fit in the boat at once, so Mr. Thomas, Marcia and her sister joined the guide first to cross the pond, while Mrs. Thomas and her oldest daughter waited their turn on shore.

Wedding dress belonging to Isabel Whittier, handmade by her before she married Chester Greenwood in 1884. *From the collection of the Farmington Historical Society, photo by Elizabeth Buckingham.*

No one ever knew what made the boat lurch that day on Greeley Pond, but the jolt was strong enough to throw all four boaters into the water at once. Mr. Thomas, his daughters and Carlton grabbed hold of the boat, which was now floating upside down. Greeley Pond wasn't deep. In fact, the group capsized in only about three feet of water. But what made their plight dangerous was the mud. Beneath the water was twenty-five feet of it. A swimmer could have avoided it and swam to shore. A non-swimmer with a life jacket or floating seat cushion could have kicked her way to shore. A guide trained in lifesaving could have hauled the others in. But poor Marcia Thomas, who could not benefit from any of these precautions, struggled to keep hold of the overturned boat, knowing that to let go would mean sinking into a muddy grave.

Exhausted after a half hour of struggle, Marcia sank to her death while the others watched helplessly. Finally, camp owner Roland York and his employee McCain arrived at the pond. Evidently they couldn't swim either, because instead of jumping in to save the survivors, they cut and lashed together cedar poles to float out to them. With what little strength they had left, Mr. Thomas, his other daughter and Carlton managed to get back to shore.

A little while later, York and McCain managed to haul Marcia's body up from the soft mud of Greeley Pond. York reported that the drowned girl's eyes were open and she was smiling.

## The Longest Train Trip

The winter of 1899 was rough everywhere. Ice floated into the Gulf of Mexico; the thermometer plummeted to two degrees below zero in Tallahassee, Florida; blizzards ravaged the East Coast. By the end of February, everyone had had enough. But for a few unlucky passengers who boarded a train in Rangeley on a Monday morning in March, winter's woes were far from over.

Snowstorm on top of snowstorm had plagued western Maine that winter. "A considerable fall of snow the past week and an almost continuous high wind have combined to render impassable highways already in bad enough condition," reported a Phillips correspondent for the *Lewiston Evening Journal* on March 23. Passengers on the Phillips and Rangeley Railroad discovered that not only were the highways impassable, but the railways as well. Western Maine's narrow-gauge railroad system covered mountainous terrain connecting villages and lumber mills from Farmington to Carrabassett Valley and Rangeley. But even by western

Farmington Village with train, circa 1878. *From a mural in Franklin Savings Bank on Main Street, Farmington, painted by Melanie Farmer, 1989, photo by Elizabeth Buckingham.*

Maine standards, the line between Rangeley and Phillips was considered especially steep and curvy.

The train left Rangeley on time at 11:00 a.m. Three miles later it came to a halt. In the first pass, wind had packed the snow solidly between the rails. Word went out for men with shovels, and a crew of forty went to work while passengers waited. The snowdrift cleared, the train moved on with the shovel crew on board. Snow blocked the line in numerous places along the route, and the trip became a series of small gains and long stops. Passengers

found themselves trapped in the railway cars, far from roads or any other hallmarks of civilization, with no choice but to wait out the ride and hope that the next drift would not be as big as the last. No doubt some of the men joined the shovel crew rather than sit idly in a passenger car.

Midnight found them just beyond Redington, a small settlement that at least gave them some relief from the wilderness. Food was taken onboard so crew and passengers could finally eat after thirteen long hours of tedious travel. The train inched on. By the time the sun came up, the travelers had managed to get as far as Johnson's Ridge, just two miles from Phillips. Here was a drift bigger than any they had yet to see, fifty rods long and twenty feet high. With Phillips nearly in sight, passengers abandoned the train and

Broadway, Farmington, Maine. The "first big storm of the winter" in February 1898. *Photo courtesy of the Farmington Historical Society.*

The narrow-gauge railroad. *From a mural in the Narrow Gauge Cinema, painted by Tony Castro, 1995, photo by Elizabeth Buckingham.*

made their way into town on foot or by sleigh. At mid-morning, a full day after leaving Rangeley, the travelers had finally completed their twenty-eight-mile journey. Weary and cold, they were treated to breakfast at the village hotel. Thirty men stayed behind on Johnson's Ridge, and for ten hours they shoveled snow to clear the tracks of the mammoth drift.

Bright and early at 7:00 a.m. the next day, a train left the Phillips station for a return trip, but it's hard to believe anyone could have wanted to go back to Rangeley badly enough to board that morning's narrow-gauge passenger train.

## The Flood of 1869

Experts say that the April Fool's Day Flood in the 1980s was the worst in five hundred years. The second worst flood was no doubt the Freshet of 1869. This flood took place in October, the result of torrential rains the likes of which we probably have never seen. The rain began early on the morning of October 3, lightly at first. As the day went on it got harder and harder until it was coming down in torrents. It came down so fast that the ground could not soak it up and several inches of water sat on the surface. Brooks and streams upcountry began to rise and, as the water got higher and ran faster, it broke away dams that farmers and millers had built along the way. The water, now undammed, swelled the streams even more as it made its way to the headwaters of the Sandy River.

Above Phillips, the crashing water from countless brooks and streams joined in a wall of force that followed its course to the town. In West Phillips, Washington Hewey tried desperately to rescue some sheep from the onslaught and drowned in the effort. As the water rose, more and more residents along the banks of the Sandy became alarmed. At the urging of neighbors, Mrs. Wyman and her daughter left their house at Brag Corner, fearing that water may get high enough to run through it. Mrs. Wyman expected to return home when the waters receded and never considered taking any of her possessions with her when she left. But there was no house to return to. As the wall of water went crashing downriver from the headwaters, it swept away Mrs. Wyman's house and barn and her lifelong possessions with it.

The waters raged on, sweeping away Royal Whitney's mill and only source of livelihood. The waters gained depth and width and encompassed the village of Phillips, the streets of the upper village drowning twelve feet below. Mrs. Soule, whose husband was away in Minnesota, took her child and mother-in-law to their attic; even there, the water lapped at their feet.

Her brother-in-law Ruel managed to procure a boat and made an effort to paddle upriver to rescue the family. The boat crashed into a building and broke into pieces. Ruel managed to save himself, but could do nothing to help the family.

Mrs. Parker and her three small children were also home alone and took refuge on the second floor of their house. Some of her neighbors quickly slapped together a raft and managed to paddle it to her second-story window. They urged Mrs. Parker to evacuate, but she kept her head. She feared her young children would be in more danger on the raft than in the house, and she refused to leave. As the men paddled away from the house, their makeshift raft split apart in the forceful current and the would-be rescuers had all they could do to save themselves. The current carried away Mr. Parker's jewelry store as watches, necklaces, bracelets and other precious pieces were scattered by the force.

The forceful wall of water washed through the lower village cemetery, knocking over tombstones, gouging holes in the sacred ground and dislodging caskets and corpses and carrying them away. The current left its debris in its wake and even deposited one corpse on the very farm on which he had lived his life. The torrent moved on, taking out two blacksmith shops and the

E.S. Dingley Corn Shop, crew and huskers. *Photo courtesy of the Farmington Historical Society.*

bridge at the lower village. The torrent wound its way past Phillips, through Strong and on to Farmington, wreaking havoc in its relentless progress.

At Fairbanks, the rushing water carried away the bridge, and in Farmington residents of the intervale feared for their lives. Rescuers in rowboats worked frantically to evacuate those stranded along the river. Elderly Mrs. Case was saved when they rowed through her front door and took her from the stairs. The water swept away the bridge at Center Village. The brand-new building of the J. Winslow Jones Corn Packing Company was not spared as the torrent picked it up with all its heavy packing machinery and cases of canned corn and deposited it in the intervale below. The waters raged on to Farmington Falls, where B.F. Morrill's spool factory was swept away. And on it raged, east to the Kennebec.

In its wake, the residents along the Sandy River were left to dig themselves out from the forces of nature.

## The Fire in Eustis

In 1903, most of the citizens of Eustis found themselves homeless in the wake of disaster. The catastrophe happened on a date that is now infamous: September 11. On this windy day, sparks escaped a defective chimney in the Coburn House, catching the roof of the hotel on fire. Eustis had no fire wagons and no volunteer fire department. Its only way of fighting the flames was to form a bucket brigade from the nearby stream to the hotel. The Coburn House was the first in a line of wooden buildings, and as townspeople frantically tried to extinguish the fire with buckets of water, the wind whipped the flames onto the nearby structures.

The bucket brigade couldn't slow the blaze, and within twenty minutes the fifteen buildings in the village were burning. The heat became so great that buildings on the opposite side of the street even caught fire. No bucket brigade could quell such an inferno, and as the *Farmington Chronicle* noted, "The villagers were helpless."

Giving up the buildings for lost, townspeople abandoned the bucket brigade after only about a half hour. Despite the incredible heat, they turned their attention to trying to save the contents of the burning buildings. Rescuers hauled merchandise from stores and furniture from houses and deposited it on the street. But the heat and wind were so strong that the material was not even safe outside and went up in flames anyway.

The fire consumed everything in its path, and villagers were helpless to do anything but hope that it would burn itself out. Finally after a couple of hours, the blaze began to die. "The wind went down only when the fire had spent itself toward the north and but open country remained," reported an eyewitness.

Out of more than fifty buildings in the village, forty of them were destroyed by fire. Property damage amounted to over $40,000, nearly $1 million by today's standards. Miraculously, no one was killed in the fire. But the property damage was so complete that County Commissioner Isaac Greene reported that "a one-horse team can carry away what little remains of the buildings."

The *Farmington Chronicle* noted that "the saddest of all is the knowledge that the families…saved nothing and are practically in a destitute condition."

In the wake of the fire, Commissioner Greene traveled to Eustis to witness the devastation for himself. He offered to take back with him for safekeeping all that had been saved from the disaster. Leaving the flattened village, Greene's stage carried only a trunk, a few hand satchels and couple of framed photographs.

## THE SPANISH INFLUENZA

In 1918, a highly infectious disease called the Spanish influenza, considered deadlier than smallpox, threatened world health. Western Maine was not spared from the worldwide epidemic and, as it ran its course, the virus killed many, infected hundreds and brought the area to a near standstill.

In October 1918, as the ravages of World War I were ending, people here were forced to turn from the battlefields of Europe to an equally deadly battle at home. As it is now, autumn was fair time in Maine, and as crowds gathered to watch oxen pulls and partake in pie-baking contests, they unwittingly spread a lethal form of influenza.

The flu swept through communities with incredible severity. "Pneumonia develops without any apparent cause, and the end comes quickly," noted the *Farmington Chronicle.* Some victims became insane and the police had to be called in. Communities were desperate for hospital space. In Farmington, health officials bemoaned the lack of a facility. The *Farmington Chronicle* reported that with some sort of infirmary, "physicians say that the disease could have been handled much more successfully and probably some lives could have been saved." As it was, nurses and doctors were stretched thin, traveling from one family's home to another, often fighting the same symptoms as their patients.

Kingfield's Stanley Steamer, 1912. *From a mural in Franklin Savings Bank on Main Street, Farmington, painted by Melanie Farmer, 1989, photo by Elizabeth Buckingham.*

Without today's sophisticated health networks, the disease took a terrible toll. In Farmington, thirty-four-year-old Franklin J. Austin, a promising young mechanic, died of influenza, leaving behind a wife and two young children. Twenty-one-year-old Esther Knowlton, fresh from a training course at Central Maine General Hospital, fell sick shortly after taking on her first nursing assignment. Within a week she was dead. In 1918, while many of Maine's soldiers lost their lives on European battlefields, others lost their battle with the Spanish influenza here at home.

# Chapter Ten

# CRIME

## Making Money in Chesterville

In hushed tones, they called them "shovers of the queer." The "queer" was homemade money. Today we would call them counterfeiters. In the early 1800s, a gang of these culprits operated out of the remote town of Chesterville for several years. There they minted their money in secrecy and spent it freely on trading trips all over Maine and Canada. Four men were directly involved in the scheme. Legend has it that many more in Chesterville knew, or at least suspected, what was going on, but kept their mouths shut. For years these thieves made and spent their own currency and lived quietly without detection.

The counterfeiters made "silver" by melting lead and mixing it with pounded glass. The powdered glass gave the coins a shine and ring that made them seem like real silver. They poured the molten mixture into molds and pressed an image onto each coin to make the engraving look genuine. The result was illicit but believable silver dollars and half dollars. Rumor has it that the gang also printed paper money and could turn out passable one-, two- and five-dollar bills.

The citizens of Chesterville kept their mouths shut about what they knew or suspected, possibly because the affluent counterfeiters were good for business in the small community. And if local people were taking counterfeit money for their produce, they would want to be able to take it outside of town and pass it along without suspicion.

Eventually, suspicion grew and the authorities descended upon the tiny community. However, suspicion and apprehension are two different things, and the criminals proved hard to catch. One time, law enforcement officers zeroed in on two of the gang members in Chesterville when they were carrying quantities of the counterfeit silver. The culprits ran into the woods with the law chasing behind them. Deep in the trees, the crooks stopped at an overturned birch stump, dropped the silver into the hole beneath and placed the stump back over the hole. When the authorities caught up with them, the suspects had no money in their pockets. No money, no conviction.

Another time, local authorities thought they had their man. He was high on a ladder, shingling the roof of a two-story house in Chesterville Mills. In his pocket was a wad of counterfeit bills. While an officer was climbing up his ladder to apprehend him, the crook took the bills from his pocket and smoothed them out on the roof. He covered the bills with a shingle and hammered it down. Once again, the officer found no money. No evidence, no conviction.

Legend has it that time finally ran out for two of the counterfeiters, who were tried, convicted and sent to Thomaston, and that this was enough of a deterrent for the others to stop their illegal ways. For a long time after Chesterville's black market currency had ceased circulating, traces of the town's shady past continued to surface.

Years later, workers repairing a roof in Chesterville Mills were amazed to discover a pile of money beneath a shingle. The bills were crisp and clean and looked as fresh and new as the day they were made.

## A Legal First in Murder Trial

When Lawrence Doyle spoke in his own defense at his trial for the murder of nine-year-old Lura Libby, he made legal history, but he still ended up in jail.

Doyle was a hired hand at the Libby farm when Lura set off from her home in Strong to walk to church one Sunday in 1862. Between her home and church she disappeared, and though search parties of people from Strong and neighboring communities began looking for her almost immediately, her body, buried at the edge of the woods near the road, was not found until the next morning. Although no hard evidence could be provided, townspeople suspected Doyle, an illiterate laborer from New Brunswick who had found work on several farms around Strong.

Based on bits and pieces of circumstantial evidence, he was arrested and put in jail, where he waited an entire year for his trial. It finally took place at the Franklin County Courthouse with a battery of attorneys arguing on each side. For the prosecution was Maine Attorney General Josiah Drummond, along with County Attorney Samuel Belcher, grandson to founding father and composer Supply Belcher. Arguing in defense of Doyle were Kingfield's Eben Pillsbury, Phillips's Joseph Linscott and Oliver Currier. Both sides must have presented convincing cases because the jury was torn between a verdict of guilty or not guilty. After deliberating for twenty-five hours, the jury still failed to agree. Talk around town afterward was that seven jurors thought Doyle was guilty while five thought he should be acquitted. Not able to come to a consensus, the jury had to be discharged. Doyle presumably was thrown back into jail to await his second trial, which took place in April 1864.

It was during this trial that attorneys for the defense decided to invoke the new rule of evidence and put Doyle on the stand to speak for himself. This marked the first time anywhere in the United States that the accused testified in his own defense in a murder trial. Today defendants routinely testify in their own defense and courtroom dramas on TV and in movies would be hard to imagine if they didn't. On the other hand, defendants can also invoke the Fifth Amendment of the Constitution, which protects against self-incrimination. Until 1864, however, defendants were not allowed to testify at their own trials. The reasoning behind this, evidently, was that someone accused of murder couldn't be trusted to tell the truth. Did Doyle tell the truth? We'll never know, but the new tactic did him no good. In fact, it might have hurt his case. This second jury agreed with each other easily, and after only an hour's deliberation returned a verdict of guilty. Doyle received a death sentence, although the warrant for his execution was never executed. He was sent to Thomaston Prison, where he died six years later, still maintaining his innocence.

## Wanzer Walks Off with a Fortune and King Gets Hauled Away

In 1885, a mysterious man going by the name of Walter Wanzer managed to steal the huge sum of $5,000 from the Sandy River National Bank without wearing a mask or using a gun. He simply walked into the bank and cashed a check. Why would bank manager Timothy Belcher be willing to cash the check of a total stranger for the incredible sum of $5,000? Belcher did so on the strength of a telegram, supposedly from Wanzer's bank, confirming that the funds were available to cover it.

The telegram, however, was a hoax. From a secret vantage point in West Farmington, Wanzer himself had tapped the telegraph wire and, using his

Broadway in Farmington, circa 1915. *From a mural in Franklin Savings Bank on Main Street, Farmington, painted by Melanie Farmer, 1989, photo by Elizabeth Buckingham.*

own telegraph machine, sent the message claiming to be from a bank. Later, when the hoax was discovered, investigators concluded that Wanzer must have been a professional telegraph operator because his transmittal was completely convincing. When J.P. Whorff, Farmington's local Western Union operator, received the message, he had every reason to believe it was legitimate.

Wanzer made off with the $5,000 in cash and was never found. In those days, $5,000 was a lot of capital. Perhaps he headed west and set himself up in business. Or perhaps he managed to pull off his hoax several more times, making himself a very wealthy man.

Twelve years later, when nineteen-year-old Albert King attempted to steal money from a bank, he was not so successful. Western Union operator J.P. Whorff played a part in this story as well, not as an unwitting accomplice this time but as the whistle-blower.

King was a messenger for a bank in Boylston, Massachusetts. His job involved being entrusted with huge sums of money, and the responsibility proved too great for him. In May 1897, King made off with $31,000 from the bank. "I never intended to take the money, but the temptation was too great, and in a moment of weakness I yielded," King later recalled.

Without a well-thought-out plan of escape, King fled to Lowell, where he bought a bicycle and bicycle suit. He then headed north, abandoning the bicycle and catching a train along the way. Eventually he ended up in Rangeley, where his behavior aroused suspicion. "The mere fact that he did not carry the equipment of a sportsman was not the only queer thing about him," reported the *Phillips Phonograph*. "He wore a bicycle suit and hadn't any bicycle." As if that weren't enough, King checked into the Rangeley Lake House under the name "Albert M. Wright" and the address "Soco, Maine." Misspelling "Saco," allegedly his hometown, was another tipoff that "Wright" might have something to hide.

After one night in Rangeley, King was on the run again, but his time had nearly run out. News reports of the embezzlement in Boylston had reached Rangeley, and the authorities there had put two and two together. As King hopped a train, telegrams were sent from Rangeley alerting authorities along the line.

One of the telegraph operators who received this message was J.P. Whorff in Farmington. Twelve years after the Sandy River National Bank hoax, Whorff was determined not to get shown up again. The telegram from Rangeley stated that embezzler Albert King was thought to be on the Sandy River train arriving at 11:00 a.m. Whorff wasted no time in contacting Deputy Charles Dyer at the county jail. Together Whorff and Dyer met the 11:00 a.m. train and picked out the suspect. As they drew near, Whorff called out in a confident tone, "King!" The young man turned his head as if the name were familiar.

"I am the man you want," he answered. King was extradited to Massachusetts. Meanwhile, J.P. Whorff went on to become a banker.

Chapter Eleven

# BASEBALL

## Baseball in Weld

In the early 1900s, the Boston Red Sox were a hot topic in the Maine woods. Howard Reynolds, sports editor of the *Boston Post*, was a part-time resident of Weld. Cub reporter John Spencer accompanied Reynolds on a winter visit in January 1914 and wrote a feature story about the large fan base the Sox had in the remote region where, according to Spencer, "they raise small apples and big rocks." Evidently, apple cider was foreign to city people. Spencer observed, "Most of the farmers that live up that way squeeze the juice out of the apples, put it up in barrels and drink them that way. One man told me it saves wear and tear on his jaws."

More intriguing to Spencer even than the apple cider was the avid Red Sox fan base he found in the western mountains. "Baseball is what they talk about," he reported. Despite living too far away to see games live in the new Fenway Park, the folks around Weld kept up with their team. "And believe me that they know what they are talking about. When I first begun to hear them in the village grocery, I thought most of them must have seen every league game played in Boston for the last five years, but most of them never saw a league player let alone a whole league team."

Spencer reported that in the early part of 1914 locals were still talking about the World Championship victories, the one in 1903 when the Sox were called the Pilgrims and the more recent one in 1912 when the Sox had beaten the New York Giants.

Hopes were riding high for the 1914 season. "They all look for Bill Carrigan to land the American League pennant," Spencer reported.

For the residents of Weld, Manager Carrigan was practically a hometown boy. The Lewiston native had played town ball in Weld when in college. He had become manager of the Red Sox midway through the 1913 season and moved the team from fifth to fourth place before October. More was expected in his first full year as manager. The Weld folk considered Carrigan "a fighter." Weld's confidence was well founded, although it would take Carrigan a couple of seasons to prove his worth.

With the 1914 season, a legend was born when a new player named George Ruth joined the Boston roster. Carrigan quickly took rookie Babe Ruth under his wing. Raised in an orphanage, Ruth needed a lot of attention, and Carrigan even roomed with him to make sure he kept his mind on playing baseball. But Weld fans who predicted that the Sox would win the pennant in 1914 might have been a little disappointed. The team didn't place first that year, but it finished a strong second behind Connie Mack's powerful Philadelphia Athletics.

Carrigan and Ruth were just getting started. Maine fans would thrill to see their native son and his young protégé lead the Red Sox to World Championship victories in 1915 and 1916. Meanwhile, Weld-area residents seemed content to hear about the games from afar. According to Spencer, Weld guide Burt Conant didn't envy any of the Major League baseball players because they had to live in cities. "He says cities are bad and as for him he'll stick to the woods."

## THE BEST OF TIMES

In 1921, the legendary Babe Ruth took the New York Yankees to the World Series and baseball fever was rampant around the country. In Farmington, 1921 was the year that local entrepreneurs established the town's very own semiprofessional baseball team. The team was founded by local citizens, backers who were, in historian Richard Mallett's words, "baseball fanatics who had a little money, and those who were mildly interested and had a lot of money."

That summer, Hippach Field came alive with young men eager to play the game and fans of all ages eager to support their team. Games were held at three o'clock in the afternoon; stores would close early and hundreds of fans would flock to the ballpark on the intervale to cheer on their team. Admission was thirty-five cents and young boys were charged a dime, to be refunded at the end of the game if they behaved themselves.

The 1922 Farmington town team. *Front row*: Leland Grey, Drew Sterns, Harry Moore, Stan Small, Jabe Cannon. *Back row*: Ken Pillsbury, Archie O. Dostie, Lou Bevins, Eddie Connors, Alec Seaman. *Photo courtesy of the Farmington Historical Society.*

Hopes were high when the talented Leland Gray from Starks joined the team as a pitcher. Unfortunately, the team's first outing was marred by wild pitches, a poorly timed bunt on a third strike and an ill-fated attempt to steal third base with the ball firmly in the shortstop's control. Gray allowed four runs and his Farmington boys could barely get a base hit. This ragged play resulted in a loss to Dixfield, 0–4.

Some of the old-timers said it was the hottest July they could ever remember, and by the middle of the season, Farmington baseball had heated up as well. When the team played Rangeley, Gray found his stride, tallying thirteen strikeouts and allowing no hits until the seventh inning. In addition, his batting was "all to the mustard," and Farmington beat Rangeley 12–0. A righty, Gray broke his left hand during the season, but that didn't deter him from playing ball. In September, the team met Wilton in a tournament for a prize of $100. Despite broken bones, Gray, "the twirler," took the mound, and the final score was 21–4. The local sports reporter noted that the Starks boy with the broken hand "was gamey to the end."

In 1922, the story of opening day had a happier ending for Farmington. With Gray on first base, hometown player Stan Small pitched the game. Two double plays and fifteen hits later, Farmington beat Dixfield 11–6. Farmington didn't falter that summer until it lost to the Taxis of Lewiston twice in mid-July. The team rallied to play Dixfield again, and while home games that year could draw as many as seven hundred spectators, that was a small crowd compared to the throng of twelve hundred that turned out to watch Farmington beat its rivals on Dixfield's own field.

Stan Small was an important player for Farmington that summer. Fans who traveled to Gardiner got to see him send the ball high over the right field fence for one of the longest home runs ever hit at Williams Field. A few days later, the *Farmington Chronicle* noted that "at last report the ball had not yet been recovered." On Labor Day, the Farmington team played a double-header against the formidable Taxis from Lewiston. This time Farmington came out on top twice, ending the season on a high point. In 1922, Babe Ruth took his Yankees to a second World Series and the popularity of baseball continued to soar. Here at home, Leland Gray and Stan Small led their team to an impressive 28–7 record.

In 1923, the Farmington boys played forty-one games and suffered only eleven losses. Eighty years later, Dick Mallett still remembered the impression these athletes made on an eager young baseball fan. "I remember thinking at the time that this is the most perfect life I will ever lead," he recalled at the age of ninety-four. Every afternoon he shagged flys and grounders for his heroes at town team batting practice and then kept score during the games. Drew Stearns played shortstop. "He was the most remarkable athlete of them all," Mallett recalled. Stearns was captain of the University of Maine hockey team and winner of the statewide pole vault event in track and field. That summer in Farmington, Stearns was courting a local girl, Aura Gamin. Any time he made an error in the field, fans would call out, "You were out too late with Aura last night!" Other players are sharp in Mallett's memory as well. There was Archie Dostie, a Franco-American from Farmington, who distinguished himself on the football field too. By the time Dostie was playing town team baseball, he had graduated from Bowdoin College.

And then there was center fielder Joe McGlone, a Harvard man who had enlisted in the army to fight the Great War in 1917 before he was even out of high school. First baseman Dick Field was also on summer vacation from Harvard when he played for Farmington in 1923. When his baseball days were over, he would become a law professor and a speechwriter for President Truman. But the most valuable player, and probably the biggest character on the team, was pitcher Sully Sullivan, who was a little rough around the edges next to some of the college men. "He came from South Boston, and you would know it," recalled Mallett. Along with a thick Boston-Irish accent, Mallett remembered a detail about Sullivan's pitching. "He had a patch on his trousers. He roughed the ball on it. This was, strictly, illegal," Mallett recalled, "but it added zing to his curve." Sullivan was getting paid the impressive sum of $125 per week to work his magic with the rural Maine team.

They were diverse bunch, this semipro team of 1923. "They went from A to Z," said Mallett, "but they all got along." Young and high-spirited as they were, they managed to stay out of trouble that summer. "They all behaved themselves," Mallett said. "There was no criticism about the way they behaved after hours, which was quite unusual."

The next year, the team moved up a notch in competitive play and joined the Maine State League. Early in that season, Sully developed a sore arm and had to quit the team. This left Farmington without the strong pitching it needed. The team was up against a bunch of very good players in the Maine State League. While Farmington still had some strong players of its own, some hitting over .300, it was not enough to stop the competition. The team had an unsuccessful season, which marked the end of professional baseball in Farmington.

But eighty years later, the memories were still fresh in Mallett's mind. Easy to access, perhaps, because they were so sweet. Was that fourteen-year-old summer the best time in his life?

"Certainly one of the best," Mallett answered quickly, and then paused. "Maybe *the* best."

# BIBLIOGRAPHY

Beedy, Helen Coffin. *Mothers of Maine*. Portland, ME: Thurston Print, 1895.

Butler, Francis Gould. *A History of Farmington, Maine.* Somersworth, NH: New England History Press, 1983. First published 1885.

Hatch, William Collins. *A History of Industry, Maine.* Somersworth, NH: New England History Press, 1984. First published 1893.

Mallett, Richard P. *The Early Years of Farmington, 1781–1860.* Wilton, ME: Wilton Printed Products, 1994.

———. *The Last 100 Years, A Glimpse of the Farmington We Have Known.* Wilton, ME: Wilton Printed Products, 1991.

Parker, Thomas. *History of Farmington, From Its First Settlement to 1846.* Farmington, ME: J.S. Swift Publishers, 1875.